How To Make
Furniture Without Tools

About the Author

Clement Meadmore is an accomplished sculptor and designer of modern chairs. He began his studies in engineering and industrial design in Australia, where he was born. In 1963 he moved to the United States, and now lives in New York City and teaches sculpture at Parsons School of Design. He has written articles for *Arts Magazine* and is the author of *The Modern Chair: Classics in Production,* which was recently published. Meadmore's works have been exhibited, indoors and out, in Australia and across the United States, and are included in the permanent collections of the Chicago Art Institute, the National Gallery of Australia, and Columbia and Princeton Universities, among others.

HOW TO MAKE FURNITURE WITHOUT TOOLS

Clement Meadmore

Pantheon Books
A Division of Random House
New York

Grateful acknowledgment is extended to Theodore M. Brown
for permission to reprint the photograph of "Crate Furniture"
as it appeared in his *The Work of G. Rietveld, Architect*
(MIT Press, 1958).

Library of Congress Cataloging in Publication Data

Meadmore, Clement.
How To Make Furniture Without Tools.

1. Furniture making. I Title.
TT194.M4   684.1'04   74-26203
ISBN 0-394-73063-1 pbk.

Manufactured in the United States of America

98765432

Front cover photograph by Guy Powers

Back cover photograph and text photographs
by Clement Meadmore

Contents

Introduction   7
How to Use This Book   7

The System   9
Paint Finishing   10
Natural Finishes   11
Materials   12

Built Sideways   15
Two Armchairs   17
Sofa   20
Two Dining Chairs and Side Chair   22
Bar and Two Stools   24
Three High Stools   26
Five Low Stools   27
Eight Children's Stools   27
Five Convertible Children's Chairs   28
Six Children's Dining Chairs   30
Study Desk   32
Two Storage Units with Drawers   34

Built Upside Down   35
Six Seat Dining Table   37
Four and Eight Seat Dining Tables   38
Twin Size Bed   39
Queen Size Bed and End Tables   40
Three Coffee Tables   41
Three Pinwheel Coffee Tables   42

Boxes   43
Four Record Cubes   45
Two Pedestals   45
Four Speakers   46

Advanced Projects   49
Storage Unit with Sliding Doors   51
Work Desk   54
Book and Record Shelves   56
Modifications   58

Reference: Permanent Record of
Order Forms   59

Tear-Out Order Forms

Centering Ruler

Introduction

The revolutionary technique described in this book makes it possible for someone with absolutely no previous experience and no tools to build handsome, sturdy wooden furniture at a fraction of the cost of ready-made pieces. You have a choice of a painted or natural wood finish, but if economy is your primary concern, paint will almost halve the cost. Plywood of sufficient quality for natural finishing is almost twice the price of fir, which can be given a professional finish using the system described on page 10.

The germ of the idea for this book is in the work of Gerrit Rietveld, the great Dutch architect who in the 1920s designed the most revolutionary wooden furniture yet seen, some of which used

packing case wood and nails and was specifically intended for amateur construction. Unfortunately nails have a tendency to work loose and the glues available in those days required considerable skill to use and even then were not nearly as strong as today's white glues.

In the intervening years there have been many books and magazine articles on furniture making, but they have all presupposed a highly equipped workshop and the skills of a professional cabinetmaker. Now, with the development of the new water-based white glues and the cutting services offered by most lumber dealers, it has become feasible to develop a system for making furniture with no equipment at all and no skill beyond the ability to use a tape measure with reasonable accuracy.

How to Use This Book

Before you choose a project, read the sections on The System, Paint Finishing, Natural Finishes, and Materials. You will then be able to decide what kind of plywood you want to use (probably fir) and will understand the properties of white glue. There are two sets of order forms in this book. One set, printed in brown on the perforated pages at the end, is for the lumber dealer. The other set, on pages 61–77, is for your permanent reference and has the parts labeled.

Two different construction methods are used in this book—Sideways and Upside Down. For every project in the first two sections it is essential to read the introductory description of the method. Although the last two sections are self-contained, they assume a familiarity with both construction methods.

The System

The first step in the construction of any piece in this book is to tear out the appropriate order form from the back and take it to the nearest lumber dealer. The order form specifies the exact cutting of a sheet (or sheets) of plywood to produce a virtual kit of parts, which, incidentally, is far easier to carry home than an eight by four foot sheet of plywood. (Be sure to get the order form back in case you want to make that piece of furniture again.) The extra cost of cutting is surprisingly low considering the hours of hand-cutting you have been saved.

Because the lumber dealer usually will not cut angles, curves, or L-shaped cuts, the designs are limited to rectangular elements, but this does not prevent the use of angled planes for chair surfaces, etc.

The next step is to mark on the various parts the gluing locations shown in a diagram. Use pencil because it can be removed with an eraser. Most sheets of plywood have a better side, which should always face outward. This will usually mean putting your markings on the opposite (or inferior) side.

All the dimensions and thicknesses given have been worked out with structural considerations in mind and should be adhered to for maximum strength and safety.

Using Titebond (or any other white glue such as Elmer's Glue-All, Sobo, etc.), glue all the parts together. Always apply the glue to the edge rather than to the face of the piece to which it is being joined. A line of glue down the center of an edge will spread out to cover the whole edge when the two parts are put together. Next, hold the parts in place with masking tape. If the tape is stretched slightly when applied, it will aid in securing the joins. At this stage, wipe off all the surplus glue that has oozed out. Use a damp sponge, which should be rinsed out before it gets hard.

Structurally, all the designs in this book depend on the amazing strength of the glue, together with the fact that in all cases the joins are mutually reinforcing. That is, to every join another element is connected at right angles, which results in their supporting one another.

Let the glue set overnight so that it is really hard, not just rubbery hard. Then you can remove the tape and begin sanding and finishing.

Paint Finishing

The following instructions will enable you to quickly obtain a professional finish on cheap fir plywood equivalent to finishes previously thought to be obtainable only on high quality plywood.

You will need the following materials:

One can of Dap spackle, No. 80 production paper, No. 80 waterproof sandpaper, one can of Enamelac or another white undercoat, white or colored enamel in a can (for use with a paint-brush) or a spray can (for direct application).

1. Using a damp (not wet) sponge, moisten the surface of the plywood to be finished.

2. Using a three-inch flexible spatula or a scrap of wood with a straight edge, coat both sides and all

edges of the plywood with Dap. Scrape off the surplus so that the high areas of the wood grain are exposed.

3. When the Dap is dry (about fifteen minutes), sand with production paper until it feels flat to the touch.

4. Paint with undercoat.

5. When dry (if Enamelac, about fifteen minutes), sand in a circular motion with waterproof sandpaper, using a pool of water on the working area

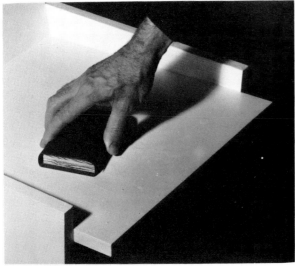

to prevent clogging the paper with paint. Wipe clean with a paper towel.

6. Paint or spray on enamel. If you use a spray can, shake it thoroughly and apply a series of light coats, letting each coat dry before applying the next. This is actually quicker than a single thick coat, which takes a long time to dry properly, and the paint is less likely to run.

Because of their classic simplicity, the designs in this book lend themselves to picking out the panels in different colors or superimposing colorful geometric forms.

When using a natural finish it is advisable to buy good quality plywood, though it is more expensive, with face and back veneers already as close as possible in appearance to the desired finished effect. It is possible to buy from lumber dealers strips of veneer which match the plywood and can be attached to the edges. The heat-bonded type, which can be applied with an ordinary household iron, is the easiest to apply but has the weakest bond. There are also pre-glued and plain types to which you add glue. These are messier to apply but stronger. Whichever type you choose, read the accompanying directions and follow them carefully. The overhanging edge of a piece of applied veneer can be removed by simple sanding; the sandpaper should be moved toward the plywood rather than away from it. Otherwise, the sanding action will tend to weaken the bond or cause the veneer to split or splinter.

Sand the entire piece with No. 120 production paper and then apply a clear or tinted finish. There are a number of such finishes on the market, ranging from natural looking oil finishes to wear-resistant clear plastic (glossy) finishes. If color is desired, it is a good idea to stain and finish the wood as separate procedures rather than with a product that does both. This allows more control over coloration and a wider selection. Various wood colors as well as obviously artificial colors such as red, green, or violet are available. The result of this process is to reveal the underlying graining of the natural wood, which can be highly effective—and which is obscured by pure painted colors. All such products should be applied in accordance with the instructions on their containers.

Materials

Plywood

Plywood is a sandwich made of three or more thin sheets of wood held together with glue. "Exterior" type plywood has waterproof glue; the glue in the "Interior" type you will be using is highly moisture-resistant. Plywood also comes in various sizes and thicknesses. You get the most for your money by cutting up the standard eight by four foot size, which is used in this book. Most of the projects here use ¾" thickness, though there are a few instances of ½".

The U.S. Department of Commerce has established standards and grades for plywood. Softwood interior panels are graded according to their face and back veneer. N is the best, but the range of A-A to C-D is most commonly available. A and B surfaces are sanded, but B can have knots. C and D surfaces can have open defects, such as knotholes. For my paint finishing system I recommend fir interior plywood with one good side (this is usually A-D). Fir has a rough, unattractive finish, but pine and the hardwoods, which have beautiful veneers, can cost more than twice as much.

If you are determined to have a natural finish, however, you should use hardwood plywood with a good veneer on both sides. There are four types of hardwood plywood, based on how waterproof they are, and grades from 1 (the best) to 4, according to contrasts of color in the veneer, knots, streaks, and splits. The main types of domestic hardwood plywood are ash, birch, black walnut, cherry, gum, maple, and oak. Some imported woods, such as lauan, mahogany, teak, and rosewood, may also be available.

Whichever kind of plywood you buy, but especially if you plan to finish it naturally, you should ask to see the sheet before it is cut.

Glues

The glues known as white glues are used throughout this book for all wood-to-wood joins. There are many white glues available, such as Elmer's Glue-All and Sobo, any of which will work. The only one that is significantly stronger, and thus slightly preferable, is Titebond. These glues can be removed easily—from the wood and from yourself—up to ten minutes after application, yet are water-resistant when dry. They also have the unique capacity of holding on an end grain, such as the edge of a piece of plywood. Since almost all the joins in this book are edge to face, this is extremely important. Masking tape is adequate for holding the parts in position while the glue is setting because, unlike the old glues, these do not require tight clamping pressures for a strong bond. They are dry enough to handle in half an hour and achieve full strength overnight. That is, the glue needs to set for only half an hour between steps of a project but must dry overnight before you apply a finish or use the piece.

Silicone seal is a true synthetic rubber which can be used as a glue for metals and other difficult materials and is a flexible filler. It is used for mounting the woofer and tweeter in the speaker project. There are several silicone seals on the market, sold as Silicone Seal, Silicone Bathtub Caulking and Seal, etc.

Spackles

Most spackles come as a powder to be mixed with water and are quite usable for the paint finishing system. The best one is a premixed spackle called Dap Spackling Compound, which comes in cans of various sizes. You will probably need a thirty-two-ounce can for each sheet of plywood.

For finishing, a good quality gloss or semigloss enamel will result in a very durable surface.

Brushes

The new foam brushes with disposable elements are cheap, easy to use, and eliminate the need for cleaning, which in the case of Enamelac is almost impossible anyway.

Foam Rubber

Dealers who specialize in foam rubber will usually cut it to size. The correct thickness for the chairs and stools is 1″ or 1½″. For the beds, a 5″ thickness should be used. In all cases, use real rubber, not foam plastics, which are not nearly as comfortable.

Sandpaper

For sanding wood and spackle it is worth the extra money to buy "production paper," which lasts longer and gives a better finish.

For sanding undercoat use waterproof sandpaper, which can be used in a puddle of water. Lumps of paint will build up on ordinary sandpaper and scratch the surface you are sanding. Sandpaper is waterproof only if it says so on the back; anything else will disintegrate when it gets wet.

Paints

Undercoats are necessary for getting a good paint finish because they seal the wood grain and because, unlike paint, they can be sandpapered. The easiest to use is a quick-drying undercoat called Haeuser's Flat White Enamelac.

Built Sideways

All the pieces in this section are built on their side and are basically similar in construction.

For all the projects with angled elements (the chairs and sofa), you are given two diagrams. On the first diagram are measurements for the lines you are to draw on the insides of the side panels. Remember that only one side panel will look exactly like the diagram; the other will be its mirror image. The second diagram is an assembly diagram, which shows you how to glue the piece together. It represents the side panel lying on the ground. The thick shaded lines are the other plywood parts laid on edge on top of the side panel.

For the study desk and storage units, the measurements for the lines you are to draw are indicated on an assembly diagram. Only the side panel lying on the floor needs to be marked. The other side panel can be aligned flush with the top and back of the piece.

All the stools are made the same way. First, on each side panel, draw a horizontal line 1″ down from the top. Then mark the position of the center brace. You can use the centering ruler, which is at the end of the tear-out section. Lay the ruler across the width of the side panel, adjusting it until the values at both edges are the same. The shaded brown square will then indicate the position of the center brace.

After you have drawn the lines on the plywood, you are ready to begin. Assemble everything on the side panel on the floor. Use masking tape to hold the parts together at the top. When the glue has set about a half hour, remove the tape and add the final side panel, using either your pencil marks (for the chairs, sofa, and stools) or the other parts (for the study desk and storage units) to locate it correctly.

Let the glue dry overnight.

Two Armchairs

In spite of its simplicity and lack of upholstery, this chair is designed with great concern for human anatomy and is very comfortable. You can add a foam rubber cushion 1″ to 1½″ thick without altering the dimensions or drape a rug or fur over the seat and back for a small degree of padding. Along with the carefully designed heights and angles, this will result in sufficient comfort for hours of uninterrupted relaxing and give the chair a more inviting appearance.

To construct the chair, draw the lines indicated by the diagram on the inside of the side panels, using

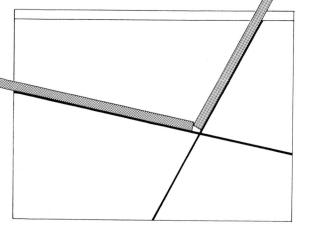

the best face for the outside.

Assemble the seat and back on one side of the

chair, leaving the other side panel off until the glue sets. The armrest is being used as a temporary support for the top of the back.

Place weights, such as a stack of books, on the center of the uppermost side while the glue is setting.

When the glue is dry, attach the armrests by laying them on a table and placing the chair upside down on them, thus ensuring that the arms are perfectly horizontal and using the weight of the chair itself for pressure. Be extremely careful to line up the armrests flush with the sides, as the accurate finishing of this connection will make all

the difference in the chair's appearance. This join will require filling (with Dap) and careful sanding to eliminate any visible sign of the join line, so that when painted it will appear as a single L-shaped element.

Note: For a stronger armrest connection, which can be more safely sat on, try to persuade the lumber dealer to make the armrest cut at 45 degrees, as indicated on the order form. Because white glues work best on an end grain, this results in a very strong mitered join. Put wax paper on the table where you are attaching these armrests so that the excess glue will not stick to it.

Two Armchairs

2 backs   20″ x 28⅞″
4 sides   16½″ x 23⅞″
2 seats   19″ x 20″
4 armrests 6″ x 23⅞″

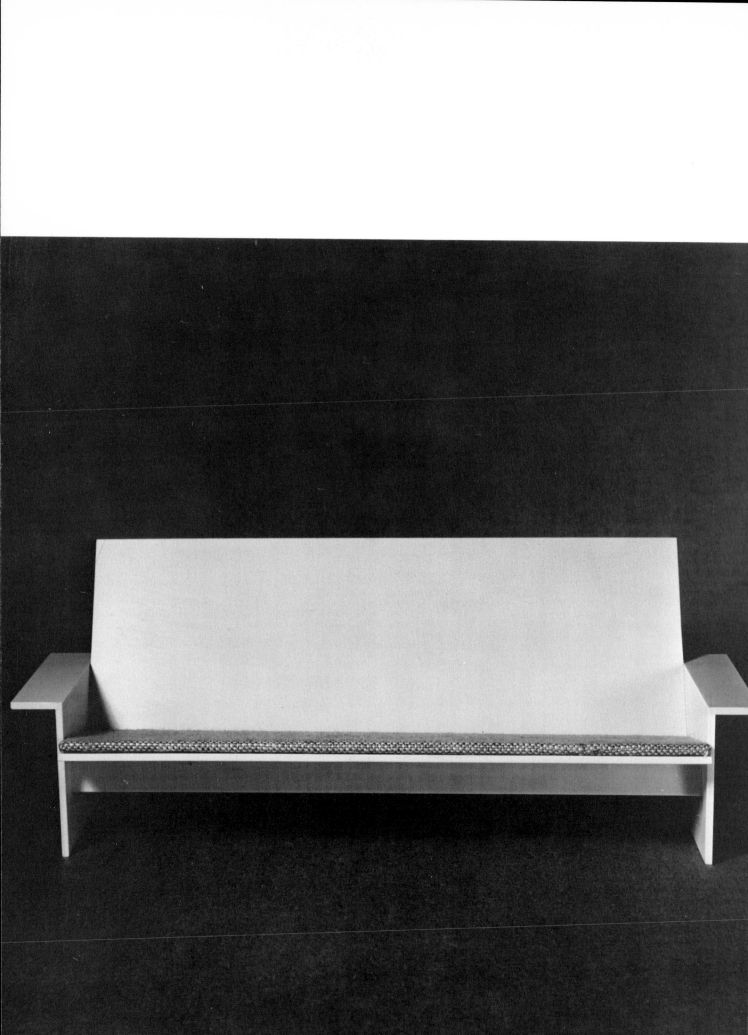

Sofa

Basically an extended version of the armchair, the sofa has a lower back and a brace under the seat to prevent sagging. Like the armchair, it requires only about 1½″ of foam rubber padding for comfort, or again a rug or fur draped over it.

Construction details are the same as for the armchair except for the brace, which should be attached to the seat before assembly.

Note: For a stronger armrest connection, see the Note for the armchair.

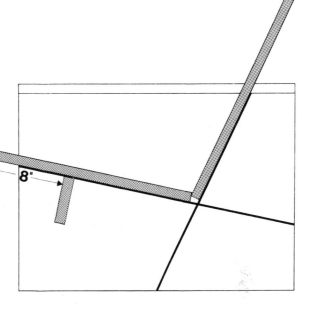

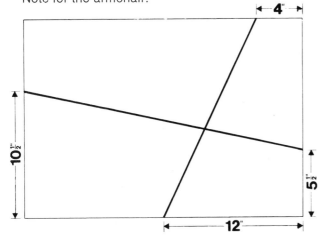

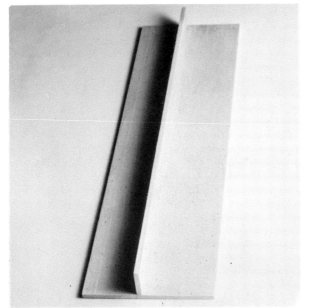

Sofa

1 back   24⅜″ x 73¼″
1 seat   19″ x 73¼″
2 sides   16½″ x 23⅞″
1 brace   4″ x 73¼″
2 armrests   6″ x 23⅞″

Two Dining Chairs and Side Chair

These are extremely strong chairs with all the correct heights and angles for comfort during activities which require constant movement. A 1″ thick pad of foam rubber is all that is needed for optimum comfort without restricting movement.

The assembly system is the same as for the armchair (page 18).

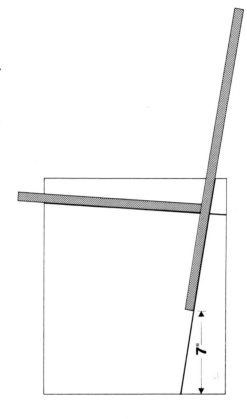

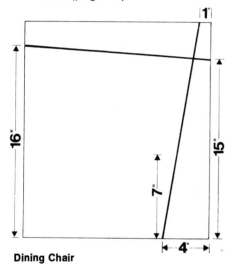

Dining Chair

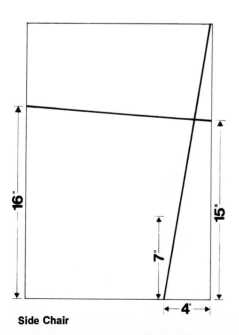

Side Chair

Two Dining Chairs		Side Chair	
2 backs	15⅞″ x 25½″	1 back	18″ x 25½″
4 sides	15⅞″ x 18″	2 sides	15⅞″ x 23″
2 seats	15⅞″ x 16″	1 seat	15⅞″ x 18″
		2 armrests	4″ x 15⅞″

Bar and Two Stools

The bar is very simple to construct and extremely practical. It has a wide footrest and three internal shelves—two for bottles and a smaller one for glasses, coasters, etc.

First mark the positions of the shelves and the kickboard. Assemble all the parts starting from the bottom.

The stools make use of the remainder of the two sheets of plywood. The top of each is 1″ down and the brace is centered.

The seats of the stools can be padded with a 1″ foam rubber pad. Otherwise, simply round off the front and back edges of the plywood seat with sandpaper, preferably before assembly.

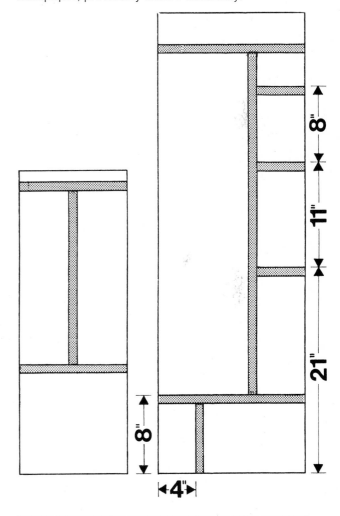

Bar	Two Stools
1 back 35⅞″ x 47⅞″	4 sides 11⅞″ x 31⅞″
1 top 15⅞″ x 47⅞″	2 braces 15⅞″ x 18″
2 sides 15⅞″ x 47⅞″	2 seats 11⅞″ x 15⅞″
1 footrest 15⅞″ x 47⅞″	2 footrests 11⅞″ x 15⅞″
3 shelves 5¼″ x 47⅞″	
1 kickboard 7¼″ x 47⅞″	

Three High Stools

Three stools can be made from one sheet of plywood. The seats can be padded with a 1″ foam rubber pad. Otherwise, simply round off the front and back edges of the plywood seat with sandpaper, preferably before assembly.

The top is 1″ down and the brace is centered.

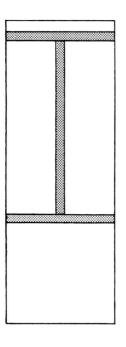

Three High Stools

6 sides   11⅞″ x 32″
3 center braces   15⅞″ x 18″
3 seats   11⅞″ x 15⅞″
3 footrests   11⅞″ x 15⅞″

Five Low Stools

Eight Children's Stools

Low stools are very easy to make. A single sheet of plywood will give five stools, which can be used for occasional extra seating at the dining table. These stools also make excellent individual coffee tables.

These are built like the high stools except that they have no footrest.

One sheet of ½″ plywood makes eight children's stools, which can be padded but are probably more practical bare.

As in the adult stools, the top is 1″ down and the brace is centered.

Five Low Stools

10 sides   11⅞″ x 18″
5 center braces   11⅞″ x 16″
5 seats   11⅞″ x 16″

Eight Children's Stools

16 sides   11⅞″ x 13½″
8 seats   11⅞″ x 11⅞″
8 center braces   8½″ x 11⅞″

Five Convertible Children's Chairs

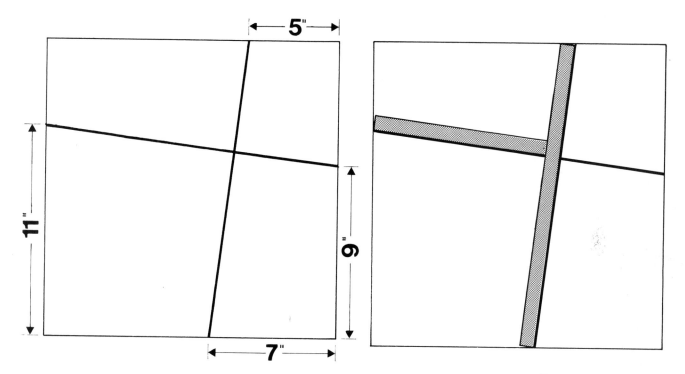

With one sheet of plywood, you can make five indestructible chairs which can be used at two heights or as tables. Round off the edges with sandpaper to prevent splintering with rough usage.

Five Convertible Children's Chairs (high seat position)

10 sides   15⅞″ x 15⅞″
5 backs   15⅞″ x 15⅞″
5 seats   9½″ x 15⅞″

Six Children's Dining Chairs

One sheet of ½″ plywood makes six children's dining chairs, which are a small version of the adult chair.

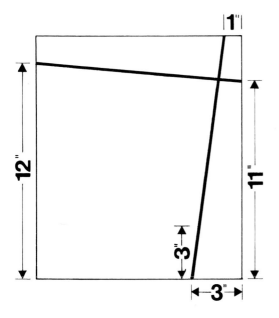

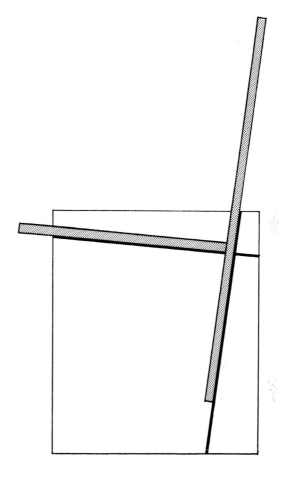

Six Children's Dining Chairs

6 backs   11⅞″ x 21½″
12 sides   11⅞″ x 13½″
6 seats   11⅞″ x 11⅞″

Study Desk

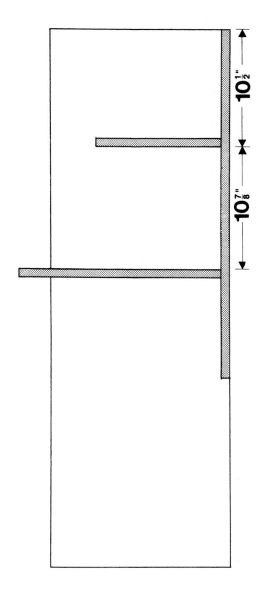

$10\frac{1}{2}$"

$10\frac{7}{8}$"

This desk has a handy shelf feature as well as a sense of intimacy about it. Six plastic drawers can be fitted under the shelf, or several groups of four drawers can be placed on top of it. The drawers, called Stac-a-Drawer, are suitable for storing stationery, checkbooks, stamps, photographs, pens and pencils, etc., and can be purchased in groups of three at most office supply stores for about nine dollars.

Study Desk

2 sides $16\frac{5}{8}$" x $47\frac{7}{8}$"
1 back $31\frac{1}{4}$" x $47\frac{7}{8}$"
1 top $19\frac{1}{2}$" x $47\frac{7}{8}$"
1 shelf $11\frac{5}{8}$" x $47\frac{7}{8}$"

Two Storage Units with Drawers

This unit is designed to hold paperback and hardcover books, as well as so-called "coffee-table books" (horizontally) and small plastic filing drawers (Stac-a-Drawer—see page 33). The spaces are dimensioned so that either drawers or books will fit exactly, thus affording a variety of combinations. The units can also be stacked or placed side-by-side to cover a whole wall.

When stacked and glued together for stability, the legs of the upper unit become another paperback bookshelf.

The order form gives you two extra shelves which can be added between the existing shelves for magazine storage.

Two Storage Units with Drawers

2 backs   20″ x 27⅞″
4 sides   12¼″ x 27⅞″
2 tops   11½″ x 20″
6 shelves 11½″ x 20″

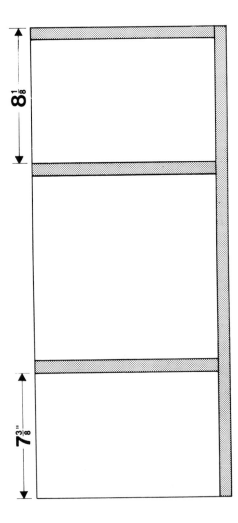

Built Upside Down

Most of the designs in this section differ only in their dimensions, so that the assembly instructions are identical. In each case they should be glued together upside down, with their top face down. Besides the top, the structure consists of two leg panels connected by a center brace.

The main thing is to get everything centered, which means getting the legs the same distance from each end and the brace down the middle of the top.

Mark out the position of the center brace at the specified distance from each end. Lay the centering ruler (found at the end of the tear-out section) across the panel, adjusting it until the values at both edges are the same. The shaded brown square will then indicate the position of the center brace.

To hold everything in place, run a piece of masking tape across the middle of the leg panels.

Let the glue dry overnight.

In all the pieces in this section except the dining tables,the leg panels are flush with the sides of the top. This join will have to be finished carefully.

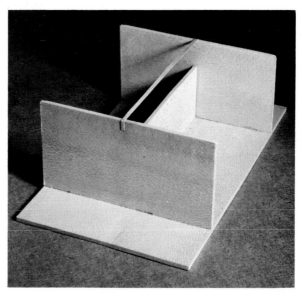

Six Seat Dining Table

The leg panels of the dining table are shorter than the width of the top and, therefore, have to be centered.

On the underside of the top, draw the two lines for the leg panels shown in the diagram. Using the centering ruler, put marks on the lines to locate the center brace.

Six Seat Dining Table

1 top   32″ x 70⅜″
1 center brace   15⅞″ x 46″
2 leg panels   23⅞″ x 25½″

Four and Eight Seat Dining Tables

Four Seat Dining Table
1 top   32″ x 48″
1 center brace   15⅞″ x 24″
2 leg panels   24″ x 25½″

Eight Seat Dining Table
1 top   32″ x 96″
1 center brace   15⅞″ x 71⅞″
2 leg panels   23⅞″ x 25½″

The four seat and eight seat dining tables should be made at the same time because they share two sheets of plywood. That is, the legs for the eight seat table come out of the leftover from the four seat table.

These tables are constructed the same way as the six seat dining table. See the diagram and instructions on page 37.

Three

Twin Size Bed

This bed is essentially a very low table and is built the same way. It should be used with a 5″ thick foam rubber mattress.

The center brace is 12″ from each end.

These thr
same tim
out of two

Twin Size Bed

1 top   39″ x 75″
1 center brace   8⅞″ x 51″
2 leg panels   8⅞″ x 39″

This b
that th
the tw
very e
preve

The c
direct

The t
page

These table
asymmetrica
they have ro

Since the po
by the others
taneously ar
are flush with

Tape the fou

Finally, befo
everything is

Qu

2 h
1 d
2 l

Four Record Cubes

Two Pedestals

These are made from one sheet of plywood and are glued together on their back, as shown below. Apart from storing records, they can be used as toy boxes, stools, or occasional tables.

First lay the back on the ground. Then arrange the four sides on it as in the assembly diagram.

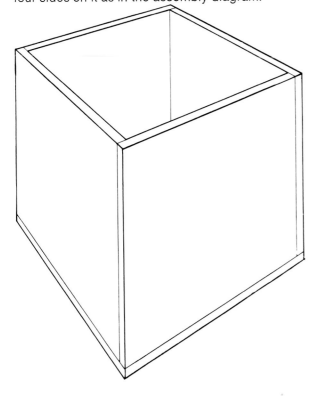

These pedestals are built like an extended version of the record cubes, except that they have no open end. They can be used for displaying art objects, flower arrangements, etc.

Four Record Cubes		Two Pedestals	
16 sides	13½″ x 13½″	8 sides	11⅞″ x 35⅜″
4 backs	14″ x 14″	2 tops	12⅜″ x 12⅜″
		2 bottoms	12⅜″ x 12⅜″

Four Speakers

Perhaps the most difficult project here in terms of persuading a lumber dealer to do the cutting is a set of speaker cabinets which need circular holes. If you can find someone to do this, you can save a great deal from the cost of equivalent ready-made speakers.

By writing to McGee Radio Company (1901-07 McGee St., Kansas City, Missouri, 64108) and ordering four of their System 13 packages, you get four speaker and filter sets for $92.00 and a terrific little book about speakers. Each set includes an 8″ woofer (bass speaker), a 1″ dome tweeter (treble speaker), and a crossover filter (to divide the frequencies between the two speakers).

The order form allows you to build four cabinets out of one sheet of plywood (two stereo sets or one quadraphonic set). These are assembled on their side, according to the assembly diagram and

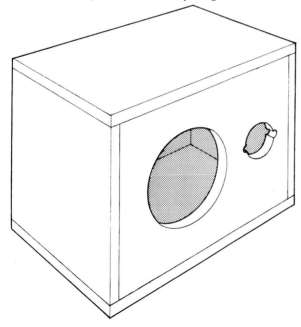

photographs. Fill them with insulation, such as fiberglass, loosely stuffed in or, better still, use old woolen sweaters. (Wool has the best acoustic properties.)

Connect the crossover filter (top left), as shown, to the woofer (top right), making sure that the red dots are connected to positive lugs, and solder. If you can't solder, find someone who can. Ordinary household lamp wire (or almost any wire for that matter) is suitable. Bury the crossover in the wool or fiberglass with the amplifier leads (from the left of the crossover in the photo) led out through the small hole in the back and seal the hole around the wire with silicone seal. Mount the woofer from the front, using silicone seal to glue it to the wood. Then pull the wires for the tweeter out through the smaller front hole, solder them to

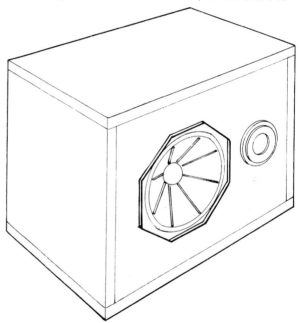

the tweeter (middle in photo), and mount the tweeter as you did the woofer. If all the joins are properly glued and the speakers properly sealed in, it should be possible to feel a resistance when applying gentle pressure to the woofer cone. If, when you press on the cone, air leaks out at the joins, apply more glue and try again.

A final refinement which will considerably increase the clarity of the woofer is to smear silicone seal on the paper surface of the woofer cone (being

careful not to get any on the rubber surround) and then, while it is wet, to imbed eight 2⅝″ pieces of 1/8″ x 1/32″ basswood on edge radially, as shown in the photograph. The wood is thin enough to be

woofer) to prevent anything from showing through the cloth. Then simply glue the frame onto the box.

cut with a scissors, and can be found in most hobby shops.

To dress up the front of the speaker with cloth, make a frame out of the four strips of wood. This should be covered with a fabric sufficiently open to let light through, which will therefore let sound through without obstruction. Paint the front of the box black (and the silver metal edge of the

Four Speakers		
8 sides	11⅞″ x 18⅝″	
4 backs	11⅞″ x 17⅛″	
	(with ¼″ hole)	
4 fronts	11⅞″ x 17⅛″	
	(with 3″ and 7″ holes)	
4 tops	11⅞″ x 11⅞″	
4 bottoms	11⅞″ x 11⅞″	

Advanced Projects

These so-called advanced projects are actually just as easy as all the others but they do have more parts and will take longer to build. Since accuracy is more important than ever, the instructions should be followed meticulously in spite of the false sense of security you may have built up by now.

Storage Unit with Sliding Doors

This unit uses two strips of sliding track molding, which a lumber dealer will cut to specified length.

First glue the shallower of the two strips to the bottom, making sure that the two front edges are flush. A few weights will help here. Repeat the process on the top with the other strip.

The center division is made separately with weights and should be left overnight to dry thoroughly before building the unit. It is a sandwich of

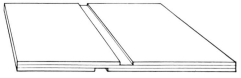

¼″ plywood pieces forming a structural brace and slots for shelves.

The unit is assembled on its front with sheets of wax paper under the ends to prevent gluing the whole thing to the floor. The top is 1″ down and

there is 17″ between the top and bottom. Draw these lines on the sides. The center division must be exactly centered.

Assemble the sides, top, bottom, and center division at the same time, fixing the corners with masking tape. Let the glue dry for half an hour and remove the tape. Then attach the back, making sure to put glue also on the center division.

Leave overnight with weights over all the glue lines.

Stand the unit up and glue the two shelf supports to the insides of the appropriate sides. Each must be level with its shelf slot. Glue the handles on the doors. Sand and spackle the front edges until they look like a single surface.

Insert the doors by lifting them up and into the deeper grooves of the top track and then dropping them into the bottom track. The doors are made from ¼″ plywood. You could use a good quality veneered plywood with a natural finish to contrast with the painted ¾″ plywood. Another possibility is to use ¼″ single sided Masonite, which is easier to paint than plywood.

Storage Unit with Sliding Doors

1 back (¼″)   18¼″ x 80½″
1 top   16½″ x 79⅜″
1 bottom   16½″ x 79⅜″
2 shelves   14¾″ x 39½″
2 doors (¼″)   16½″ x 40⅛″
2 sides   16½″ x 23⅞″
1 center division   15⅜″ x 17″,
(¼″, five parts)   8″ x 15⅜″, 8″ x 15⅜″
                            10″ x 15⅜″, 6″ x 15⅜″
2 shelf supports (¼″)   8″ x 15⅜″, 10″ x 15⅜″

Book and Record Shelves

The book and record shelf unit is constructed from three sheets of ½" plywood for the supporting elements and two sheets of ¾" for the shelves. These units are simply stacked to form record racks (or large art book or magazine holders), hardcover book shelves, and paperback shelves.

The parts can be used to make either a single large unit, 8' x 8', or several low units. The U-shaped support elements divide the shelves into three 32" spans, which are structurally sound for supporting a full load of books without sagging.

The only gluing necessary is in assembling the three panels which make up each support unit,

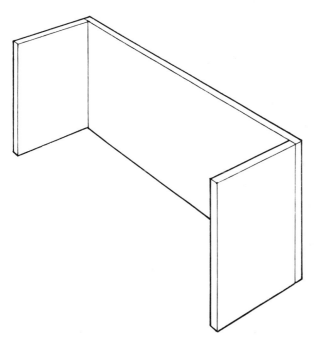

and of course the panels in each record (or magazine) holder.

If the whole structure tends to lean forward due to an uneven floor, the units should be stacked progressively further back to maintain contact with the wall. If you still have trouble, get someone to anchor it to the wall at two points about six feet up.

Book and Record Shelves	
3 shelves (¾")	13⅞" x 96"
5 shelves (¾")	10" x 96"
6 backs	13" x 32"
6 backs	11½" x 32"
6 backs	9½" x 32"
30 dividers	12⅝" x 13"
12 sides	7⅞" x 11½"
12 sides	7⅞" x 9½"

Modifications

High Back Dining and Side Chairs

For a more formal effect, the backs can be increased in height by changing the three 25½″ dimensions to 29″.

Short Desk

The work desk can be shortened to any size by reducing the long dimension by the desired amount. If you are making it less than four feet, you will need to eliminate one of the drawer units to allow enough leg room.

Typing Table

The four seat dining table can be modified for typing by marking a cut at 24″ in the 32″ piece, using the 12⅝″ x 48″ leftover section as a center brace, and setting the top 1″ below the sides.

This table is built on its side.

Convertible Dining/Coffee Table

By changing both 23⅞″ dimensions of the six seat dining table to 18″ and leaving the top unattached, you can use the base for two different heights: 26¼″ or 18¾″. Build this on its top, but put wax paper under the leg panels so that they won't be glued on.

Two strips can be glued down the center of the underside of the top to fit over the brace when the table is used as a dining table. These can be made from any scrap the lumber dealer has and should be 45½″ long.

Magazine Shelves Under Coffee Tables

The short and long coffee tables (page 41) can be modified by gluing extra pieces, 28⅛″ x 28⅛″ for the short one and 28⅛″ x 39½″ for the long one, under the brace. These can be ½″ plywood cut from scraps at the lumber dealer's.

Love Seat

Shorten the sofa by changing the 73¼″ dimension to 48″.

High and Low Back Armchairs

By reducing the back height of one of the armchairs, the other one can be given a headrest with the extra wood. Between the two 19″ dimensions, insert three new measurements: 24½″, 20″, and 13″. (Don't forget to cross out the now unused cut.) Also specify that the cut between the 20″ and 13″ be at a ten degree tilt from the vertical (most saw blades can be tilted, though it may take some persuasion). This angled cut enables you to glue the back together at the correct angle for the head support.

Decoration

Paint each plane a different color.

Paint geometric designs.

Make cut-out shapes from a self-adhesive plastic, such as Con-Tact.

Reference
Permanent Record of Order Forms

Two Armchairs   61
Sofa   61
Two Dining Chairs and Side Chair   62
Bar and Two Stools   63
Three High Stools   64
Five Low Stools   64
Eight Children's Stools   65
Five Convertible Children's Chairs   65
Six Children's Dining Chairs   66
Study Desk   66
Two Storage Units with Drawers   67
Six Seat Dining Table   67
Four and Eight Seat Dining Tables   68
Twin Size Bed   69
Queen Size Bed and End Tables   70
Three Coffee Tables   71
Three Pinwheel Coffee Tables   72
Four Record Cubes   73
Two Pedestals   73
Four Speakers   74
Storage Unit with Sliding Doors   75
Work Desk   76
Book and Record Shelves   76-7

One 8′ x 4′ sheet of ¾″ plywood

One 8′ x 4′ sheet of ¾″ plywood

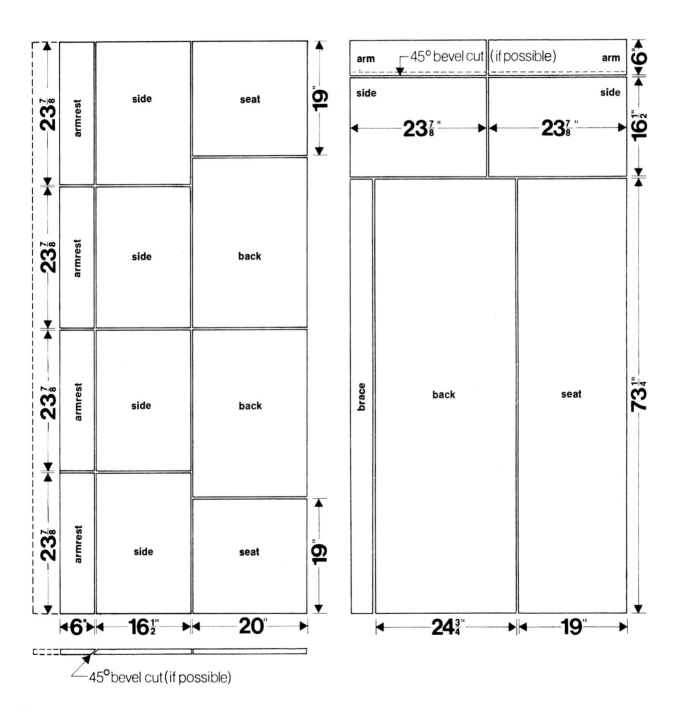

Two Armchairs

Sofa

One 8′ x 4′ sheet of ¾″ plywood

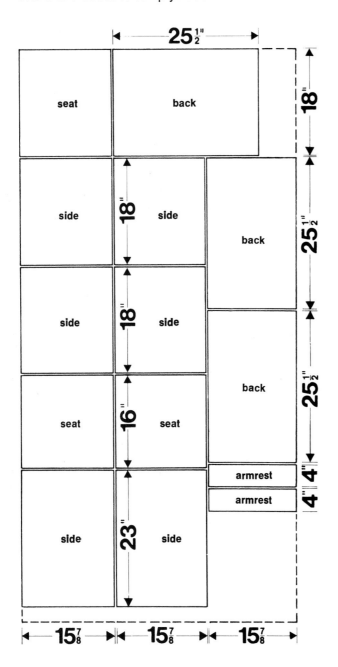

Two Dining Chairs and Side Chair

Two 8′ x 4′ sheets of ¾″ plywood

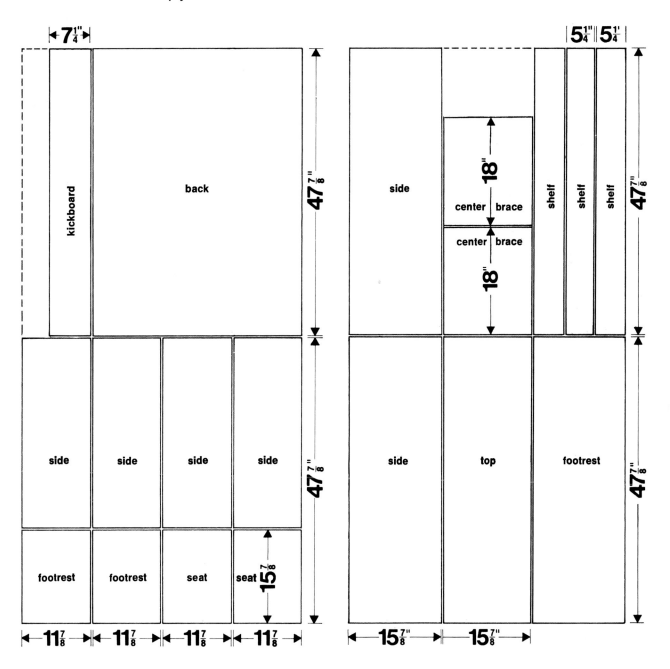

Bar and Two Stools

One 8′ x 4′ sheet of ¾″ plywood   One 8′ x 4′ sheet of ¾″ plywood

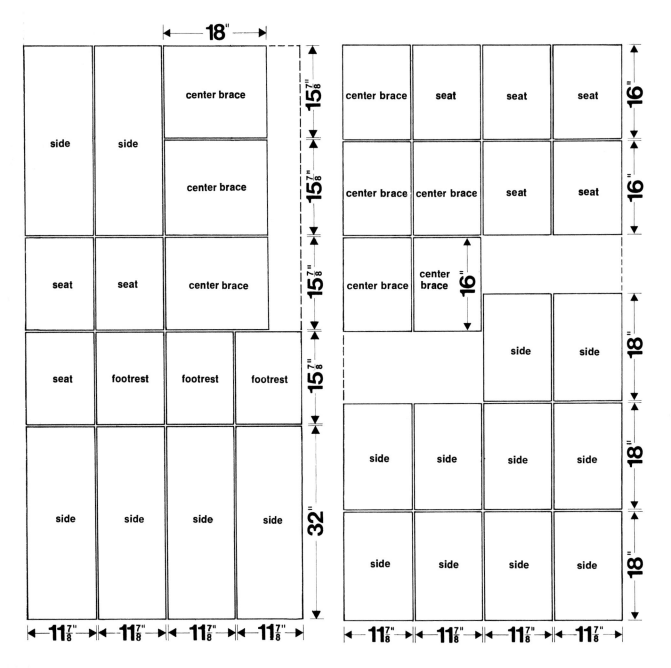

Three High Stools   **Five Low Stools**

One 8′ x 4′ sheet of ½″ plywood

One 8′ x 4′ sheet of ¾″ plywood

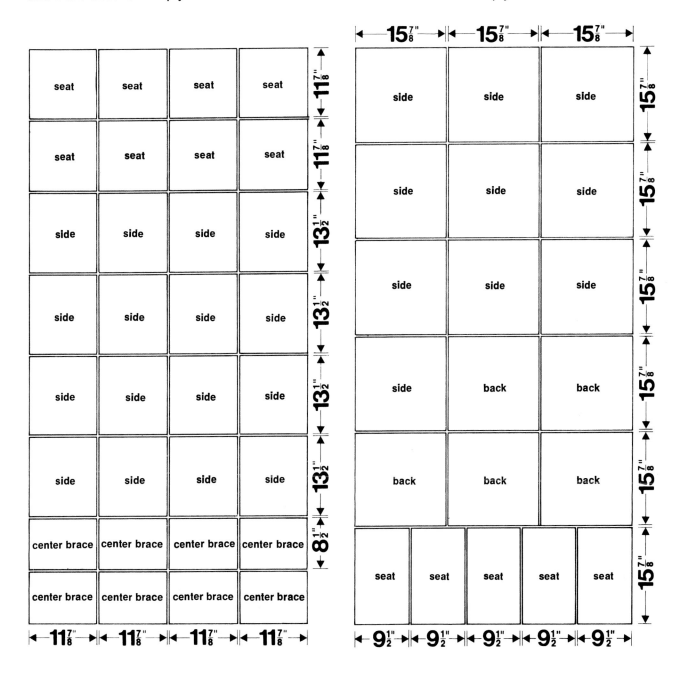

Eight Children's Stools

Five Convertible Children's Chairs

One 8′ x 4′ sheet of ½″ plywood   One 8′ x 4′ sheet of ¾″ plywood

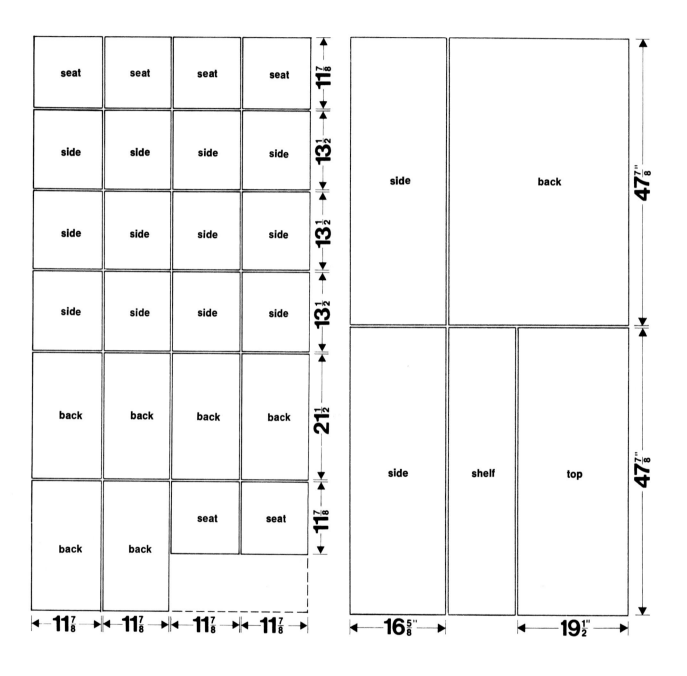

Six Children's Dining Chairs   **Study Desk**

One 8' x 4' sheet of ¾" plywood

One 8' x 4' sheet of ¾" plywood

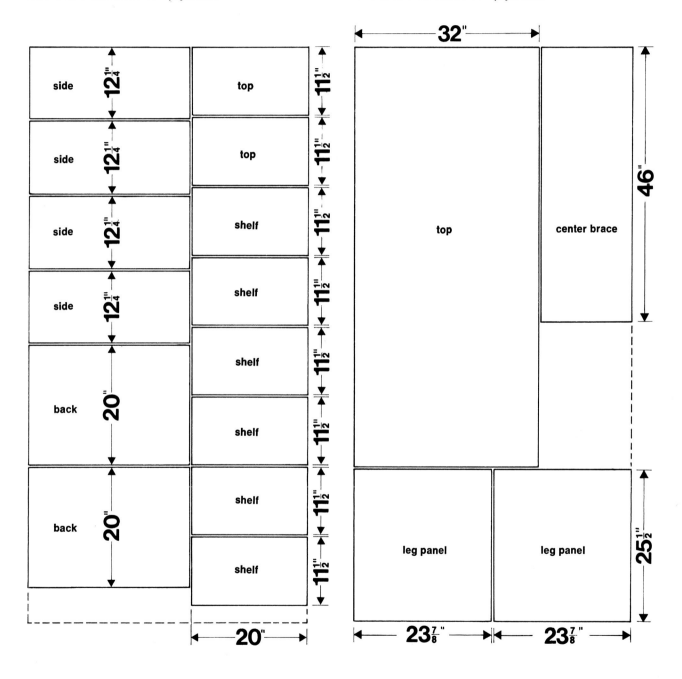

Two Storage Units with Drawers

Six Seat Dining Table

Two 8′ x 4′ sheets of ¾″ plywood

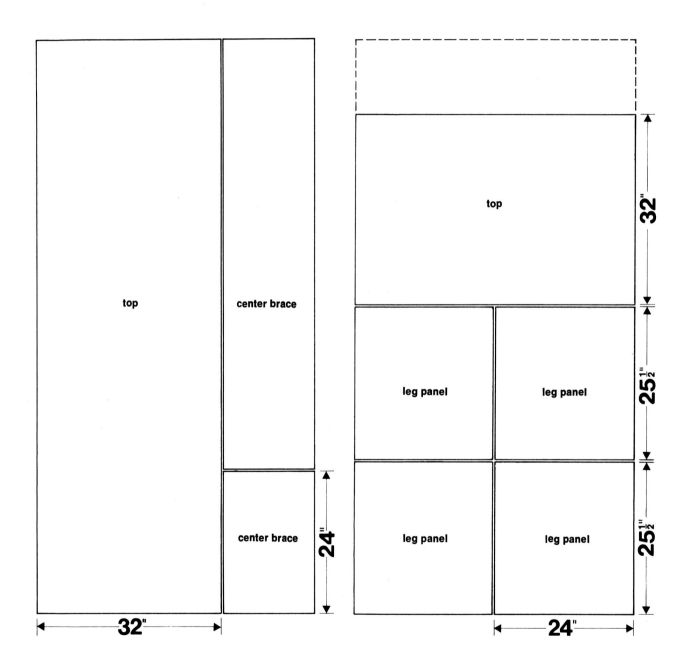

Four and Eight Seat Dining Tables

One 8' x 4' sheet of ¾" plywood

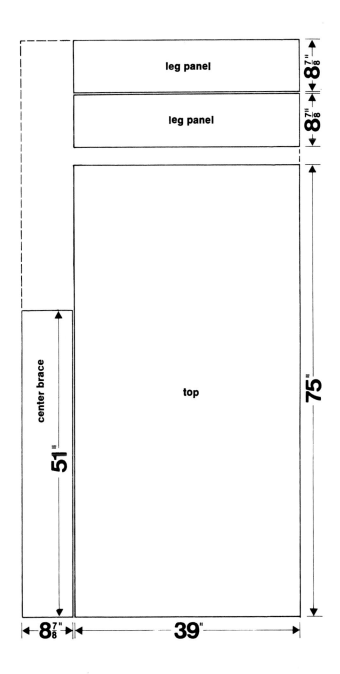

leg panel

leg panel

$8\frac{7}{8}$"

$8\frac{7}{8}$"

center brace

top

75"

51"

$8\frac{7}{8}$"

39"

Twin Size Bed

Two 8' x 4' sheets of ¾" plywood

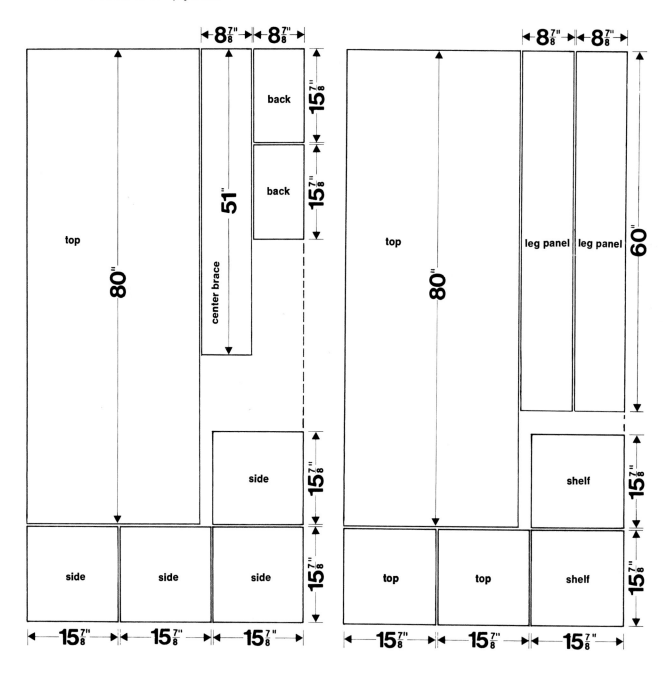

Queen Size Bed and End Tables

Two 8' x 4' sheets of ¾" plywood

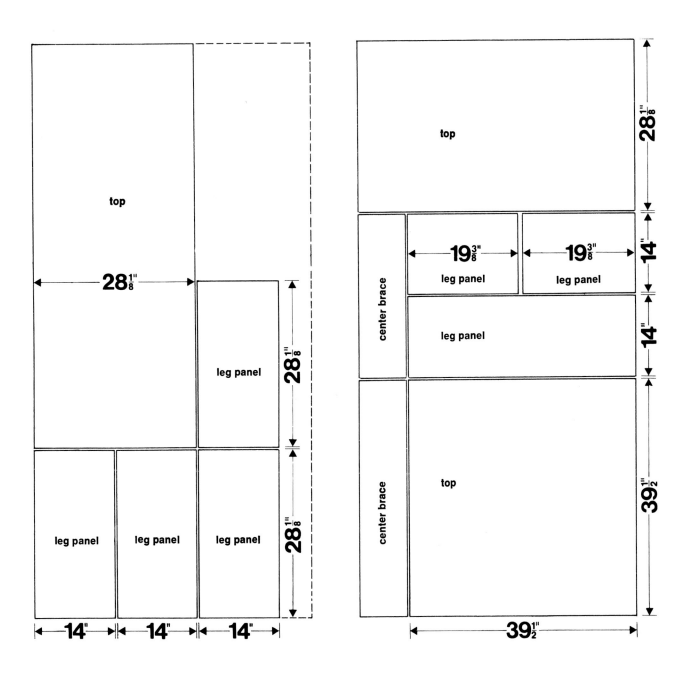

Three Coffee Tables

Two 8′ x 4′ sheets of ¾″ plywood

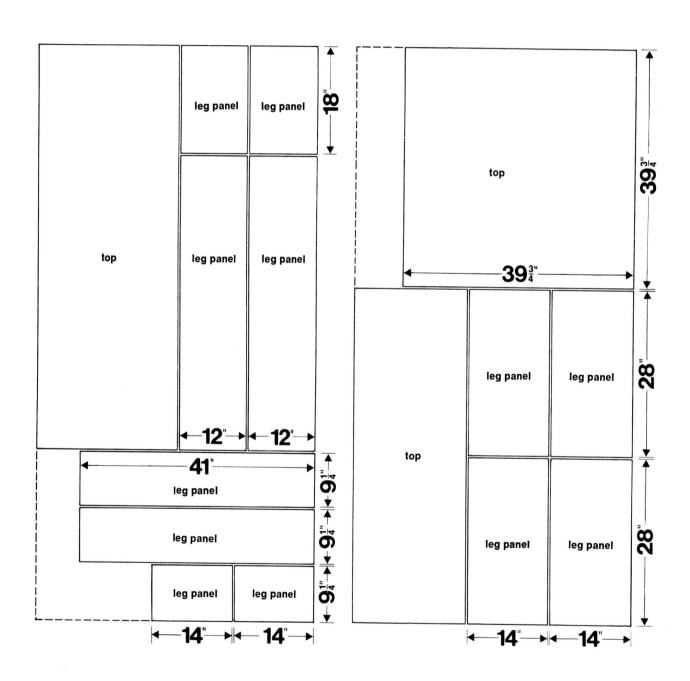

Three Pinwheel Coffee Tables

One 8′ x 4′ sheet of ½″ plywood

One 8′ x 4′ sheet of ½″ plywood

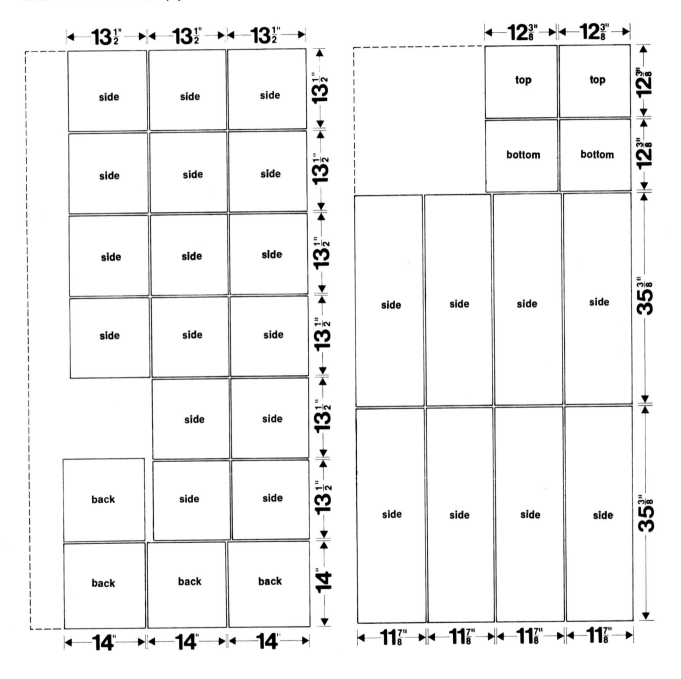

Four Record Cubes

Two Pedestals

One 8' x 4' sheet of ¾" plywood

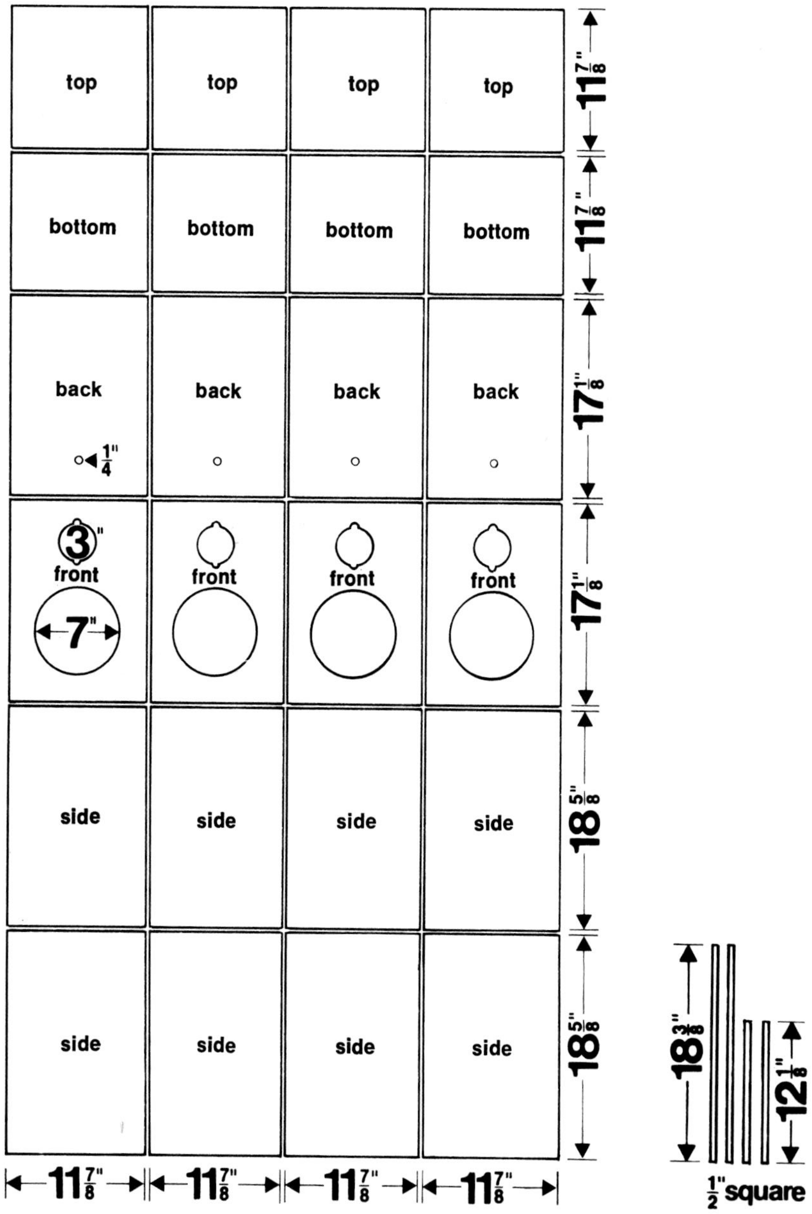

top	top	top	top
bottom	bottom	bottom	bottom
back	back	back	back
front	front	front	front
side	side	side	side
side	side	side	side

$11\frac{7}{8}$"
$11\frac{7}{8}$"
$17\frac{1}{8}$"
$17\frac{1}{8}$"
$18\frac{5}{8}$"
$18\frac{5}{8}$"

$\frac{1}{4}$"

(3)" front
◄ 7" ►

$11\frac{7}{8}$" | $11\frac{7}{8}$" | $11\frac{7}{8}$" | $11\frac{7}{8}$"

$18\frac{3}{8}$"
$12\frac{1}{8}$"
$\frac{1}{2}$" square

Four Speakers

One 8' x 4' sheet of ¼" plywood

One 8' x 4' sheet of ¾" plywood

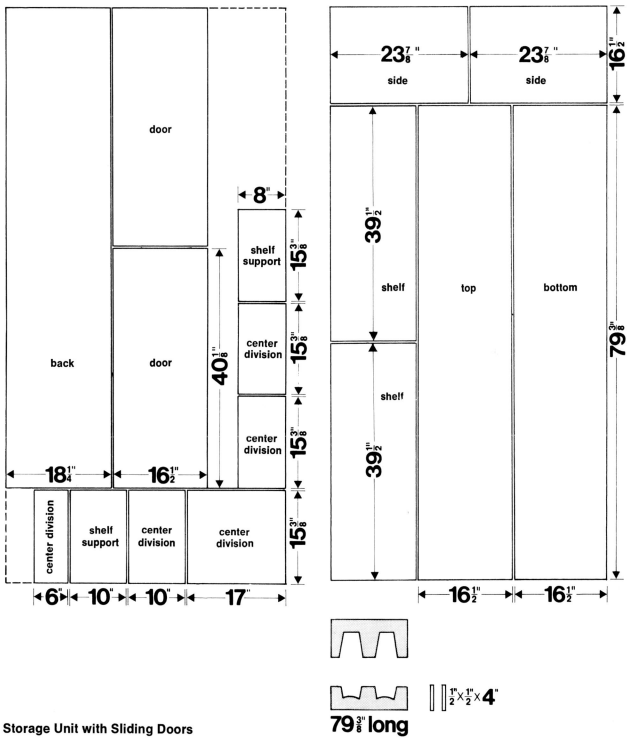

Storage Unit with Sliding Doors

One 8′ x 4′ sheet of ¾″ plywood

Three 8′ x 4′ sheets of ½″ plywood

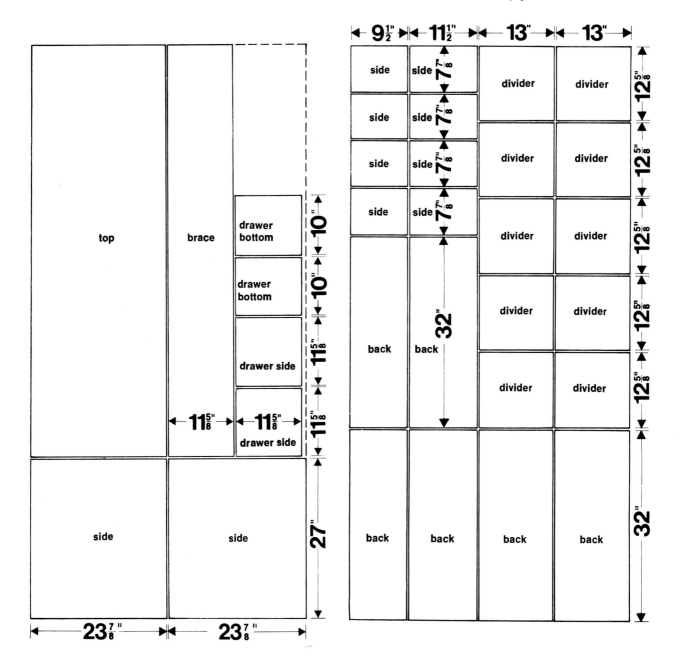

Work Desk

Book and Record Shelves

Two 8′ x 4′ sheets of ¾″ plywood

|← 13⅞″ →|← 10″ →|← 10″ →|← 10″ →|

shelf   shelf   shelf   shelf

|← 13⅞″ →|← 13⅞″ →|← 10″ →|← 10″ →|

shelf   shelf   shelf   shelf

Book and Record Shelves

Tear-Out Order Forms

These order forms are for the lumber dealer. The only other information he will need to know is what grade of plywood you want. Assuming that you are using a paint finish, I recommend fir plywood (A-D), which is the cheapest.

Modifications can be incorporated by changing the appropriate dimensions on these forms or by making dotted lines solid lines. Use pencil so that you can still build the unmodified version in the future.

Be sure to get your order form back from the lumber dealer in case you decide to use it again. If it is lost, however, you can copy the one in the Reference section on pages 61–77.

Order No. 1: Two Armchairs

Order No. 2: Sofa

Order No. 3: Two Dining Chairs and Side Chair

Order No. 4: Bar and Two Stools

Order No. 5: Three High Stools

Order No. 6: Five Low Stools

Order No. 7: Eight Children's Stools

Order No. 8: Five Convertible Children's Chairs

Order No. 9: Six Children's Dining Chairs

Order No. 10: Study Desk

Order No. 11: Two Storage Units with Drawers

Order No. 12: Six Seat Dining Table

Order No. 13: Four and Eight Seat Dining Tables

Order No. 14: Twin Size Bed

Order No. 15: Queen Size Bed and End Tables

Order No. 16: Three Coffee Tables

Order No. 17: Three Pinwheel Coffee Tables

Order No. 18: Four Record Cubes

Order No. 19: Two Pedestals

Order No. 20: Four Speakers

Order No. 21: Storage Unit with Sliding Doors

Order No. 22: Work Desk

Order No. 23: Book and Record Shelves

Order No. 1: Two Armchairs

Order No. 1

Name

Address

Telephone

Please supply
one 8′ x 4′ sheet of ¾″ plywood cut as shown

23⅞
23⅞
23⅞
23⅞
19"
19"
6"
16½"
20"
45° bevel cut (if possible)

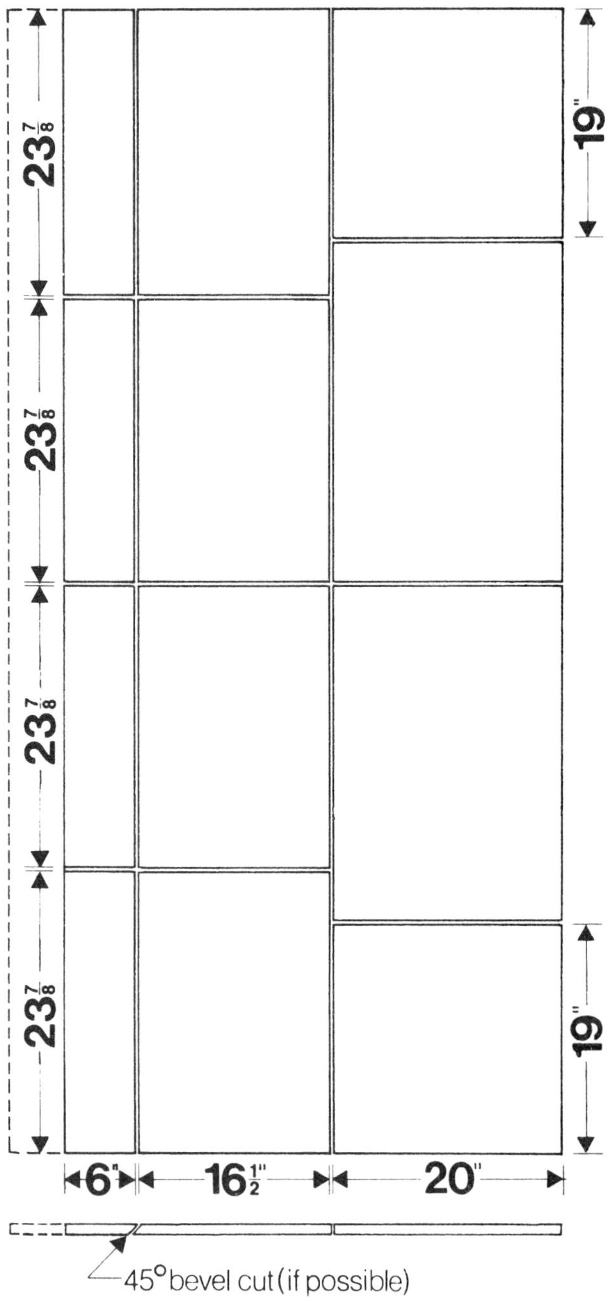

Order No. 2

Name _____

Address _____

_____

Telephone _____

Please supply
one 8′ x 4′ sheet of ¾″ plywood cut as shown

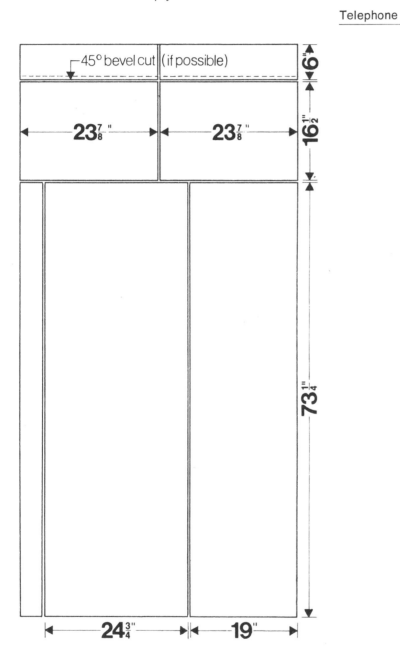

Order No. 3

Please supply
one 8′ x 4′ sheet of ¾″ plywood cut as shown

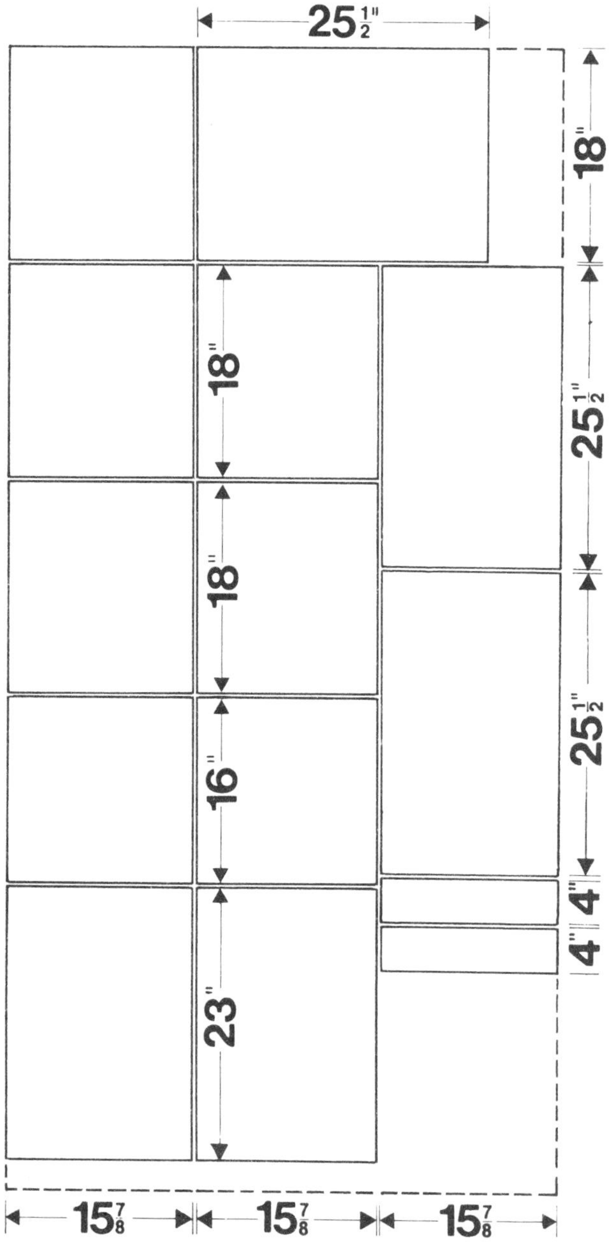

Name _____

Address _____

_____

Telephone _____

$25\frac{1}{2}$″

18″

18″

18″

16″

23″

$25\frac{1}{2}$″

$25\frac{1}{2}$″

4″ 4″

$15\frac{7}{8}$ $15\frac{7}{8}$ $15\frac{7}{8}$

Order No. 4

Please supply

two 8′ x 4′ sheets of ¾″ plywood cut as shown

Name _____

Address _____

_____

Telephone _____

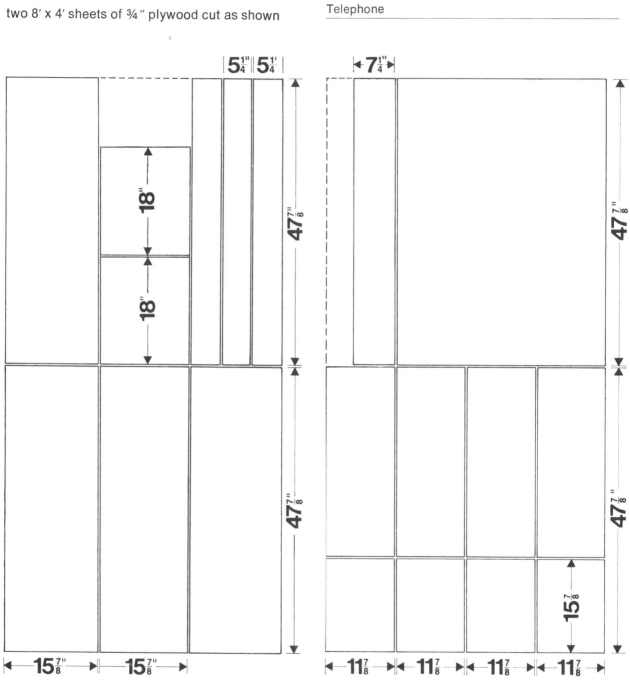

Order No. 5

Name _____

Address _____

_____

Telephone _____

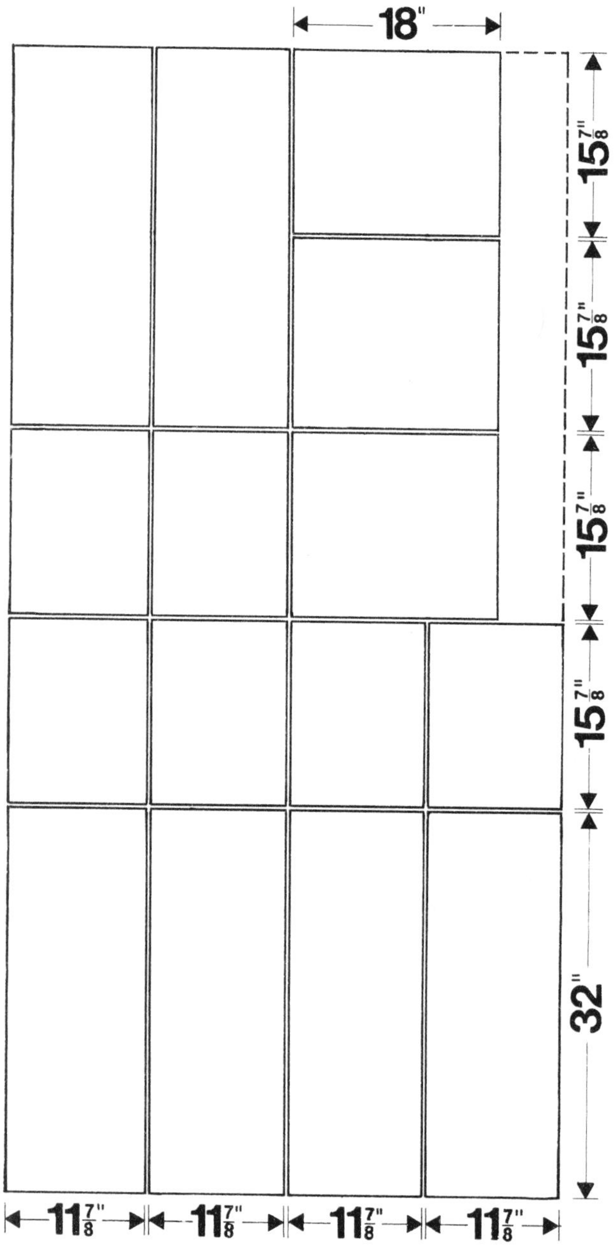

Please supply
one 8′ x 4′ sheet of ¾″ plywood cut as shown

Order No. 6

Please supply
one 8′ x 4′ sheet of ¾″ plywood cut as shown

Name _____

Address _____

_____

Telephone _____

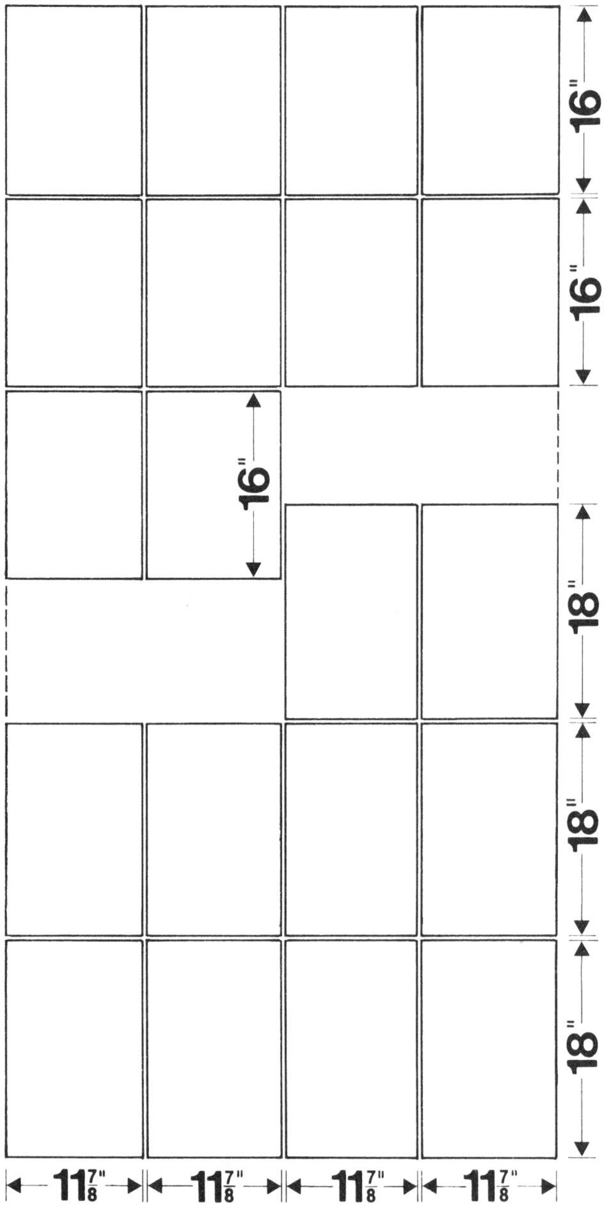

Order No. 7

Name

Address

Please supply
one 8′ x 4′ sheet of ½″ plywood cut as shown

Telephone

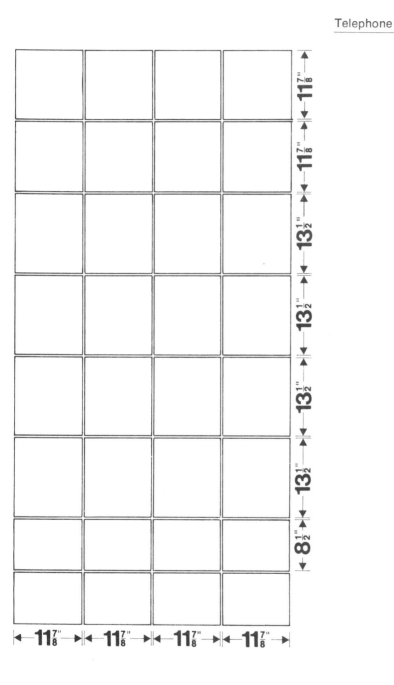

Order No. 8

Name _____

Address _____

_____

Telephone _____

Please supply
one 8′ x 4′ sheet of ¾″ plywood cut as shown

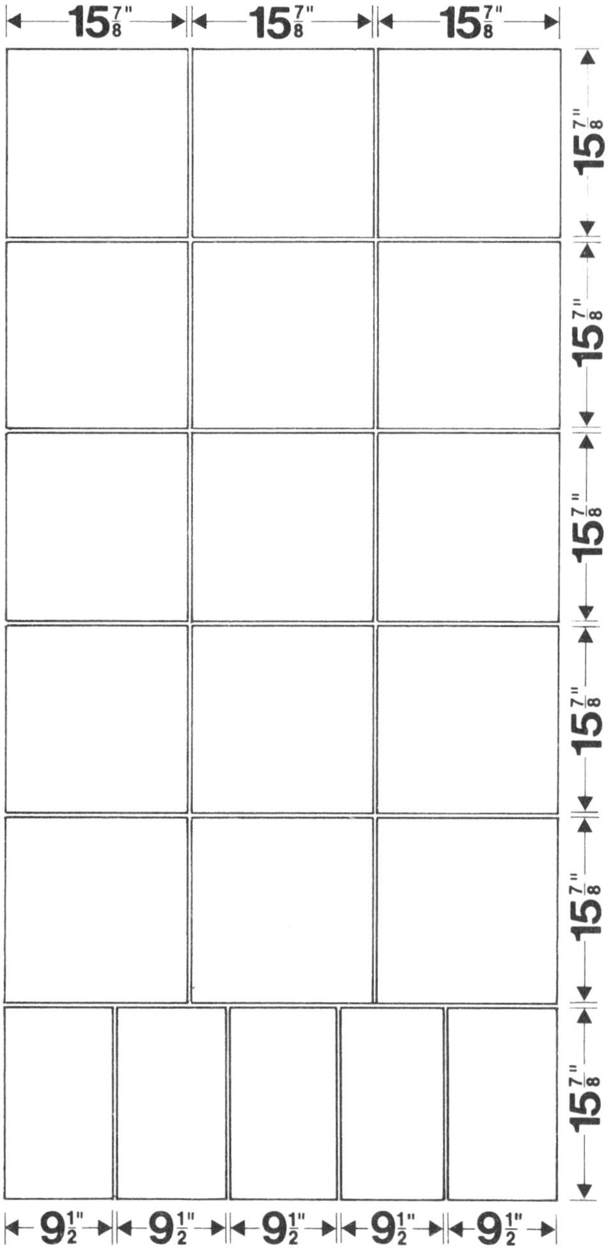

Order No. 9

Name _____

Address _____

_____

Please supply
one 8′ x 4′ sheet of ½″ plywood cut as shown

Telephone _____

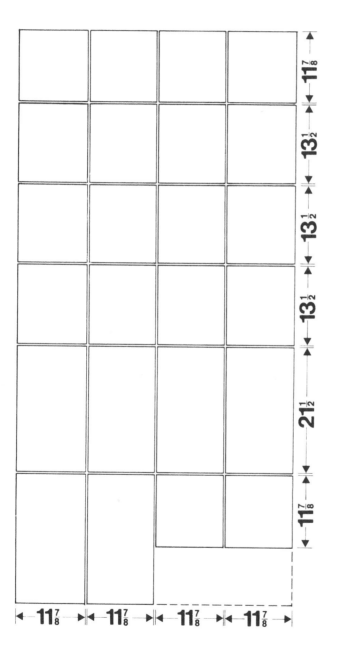

Order No. 10

Name _____

Address _____

_____

Telephone _____

Please supply
one 8′ x 4′ sheet of ¾″ plywood cut as shown

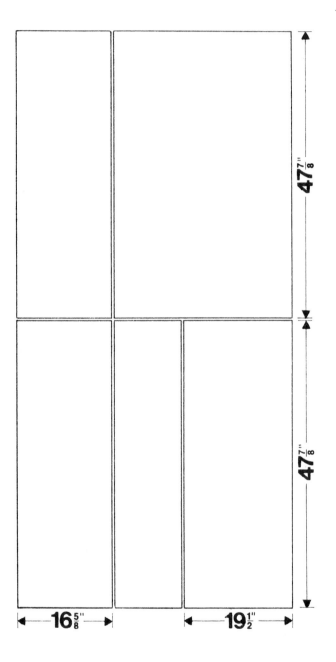

Order No. 11

Please supply
one 8′ x 4′ sheet of ¾″ plywood cut as shown

Name _____

Address _____

_____

Telephone _____

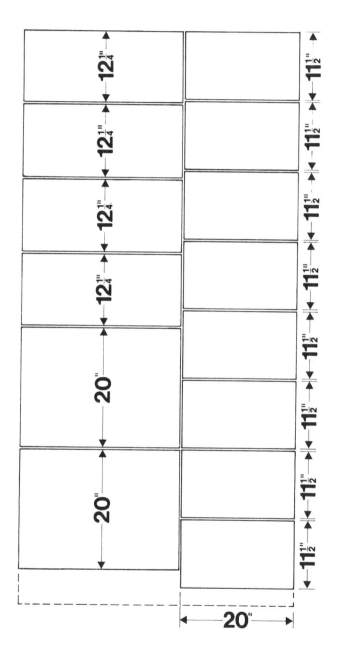

Order No. 12

Please supply

one 8′ x 4′ sheet of ¾″ plywood cut as shown

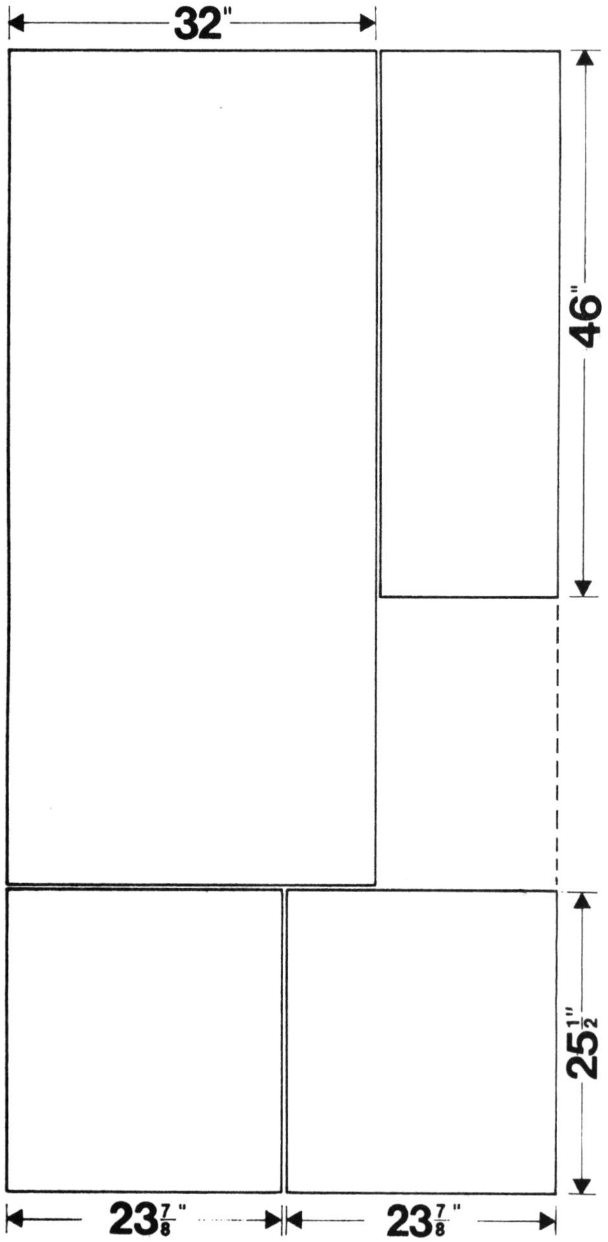

Name

Address

Telephone

$32''$

$46''$

$25\frac{1}{2}''$

$23\frac{7}{8}''$ $23\frac{7}{8}''$

Order No. 13

Please supply
two 8′ x 4′ sheets of ¾″ plywood cut as shown

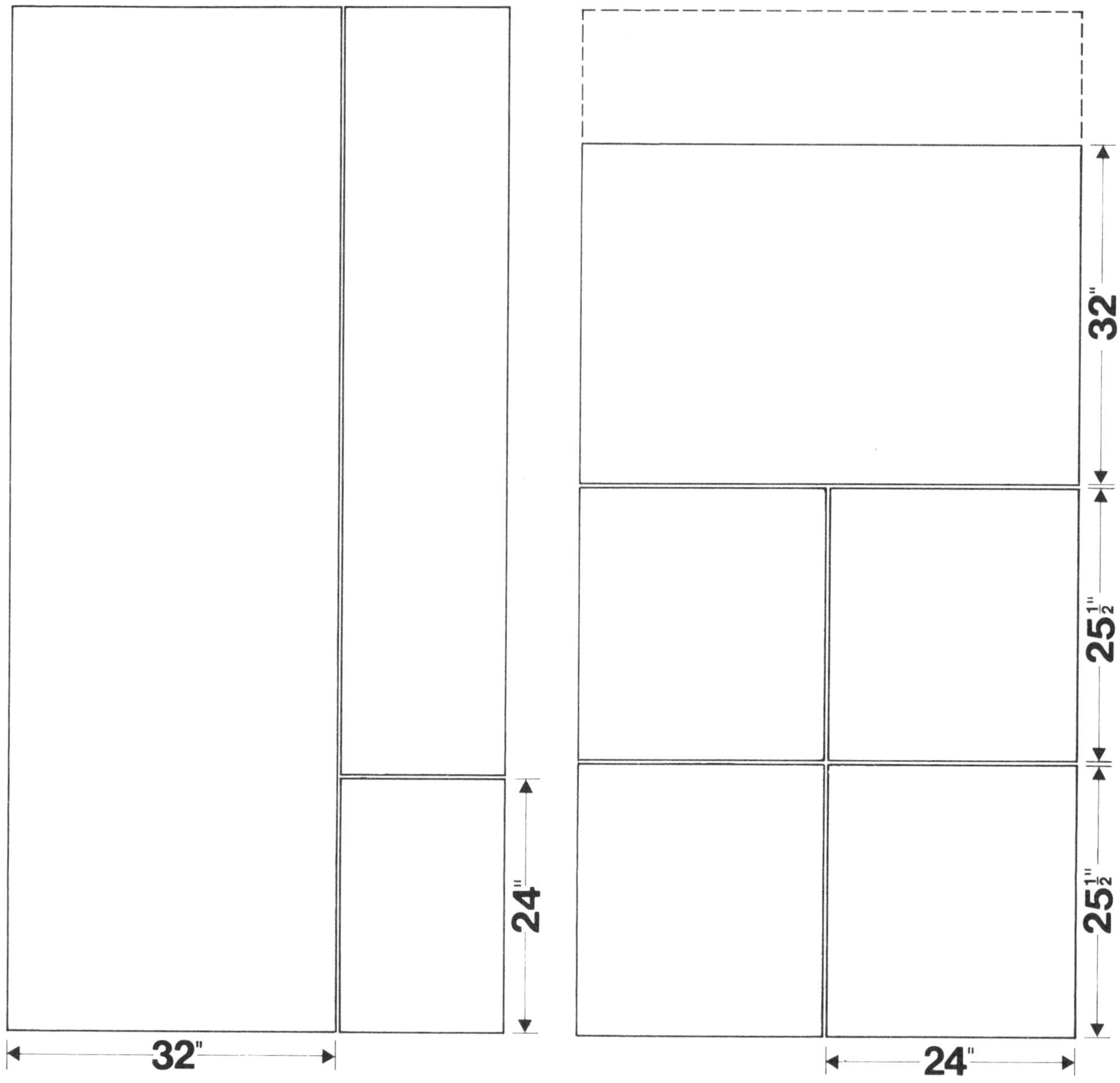

Name

Address

Telephone

32″

24″

32″

25½″

25½″

24″

Order No. 14

Please supply

one 8' x 4' sheet of ¾" plywood cut as shown

Name _____

Address _____

_____

Telephone _____

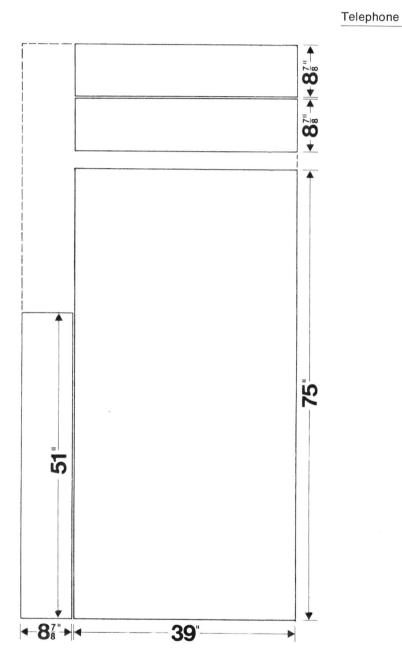

Order No. 15

Please supply
two 8' x 4' sheets of ¾" plywood cut as shown

Name

Address

Telephone

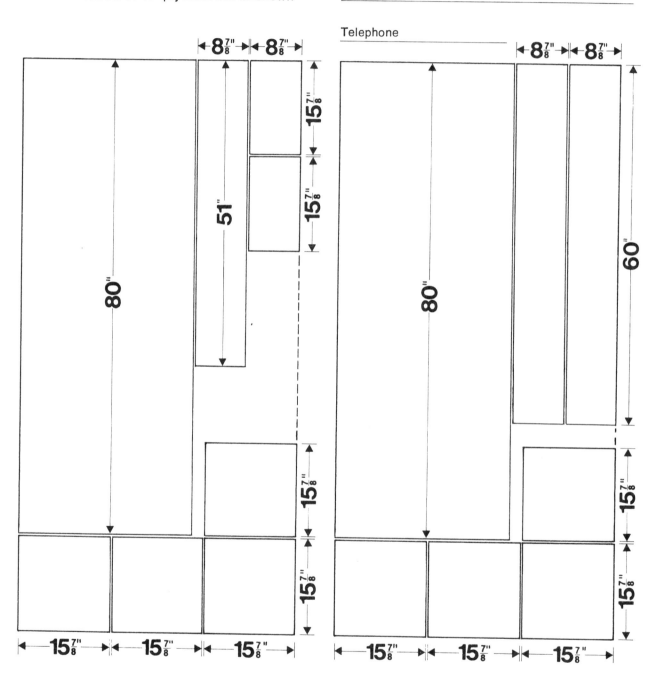

Order No. 16

Name _____

Address _____

_____

Telephone _____

Please supply
two 8′ x 4′ sheets of ¾″ plywood cut as shown

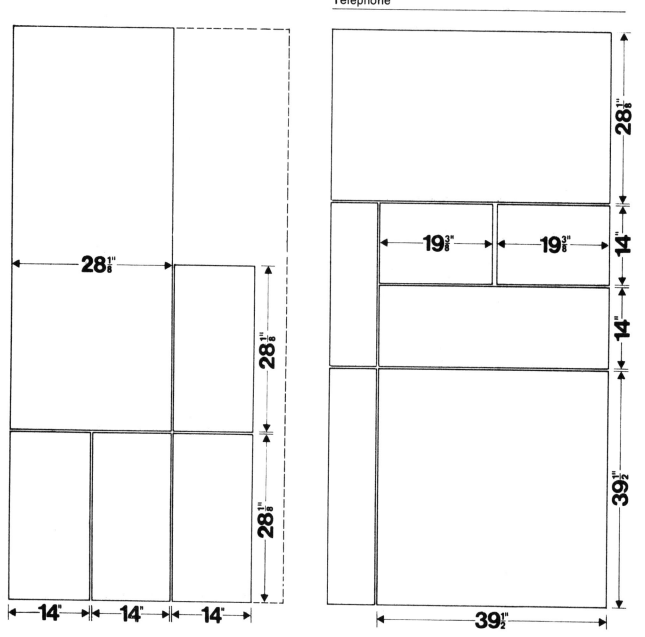

Order No. 17

Name

Address

Telephone

Please supply
two 8′ x 4′ sheets of ¾″ plywood cut as shown

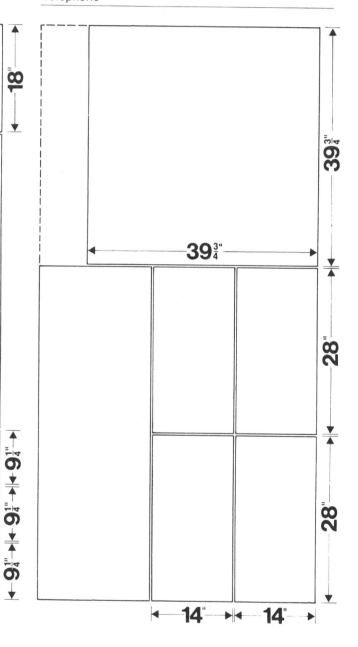

Order No. 18

Please supply
one 8′ x 4′ sheet of ½″ plywood cut as shown

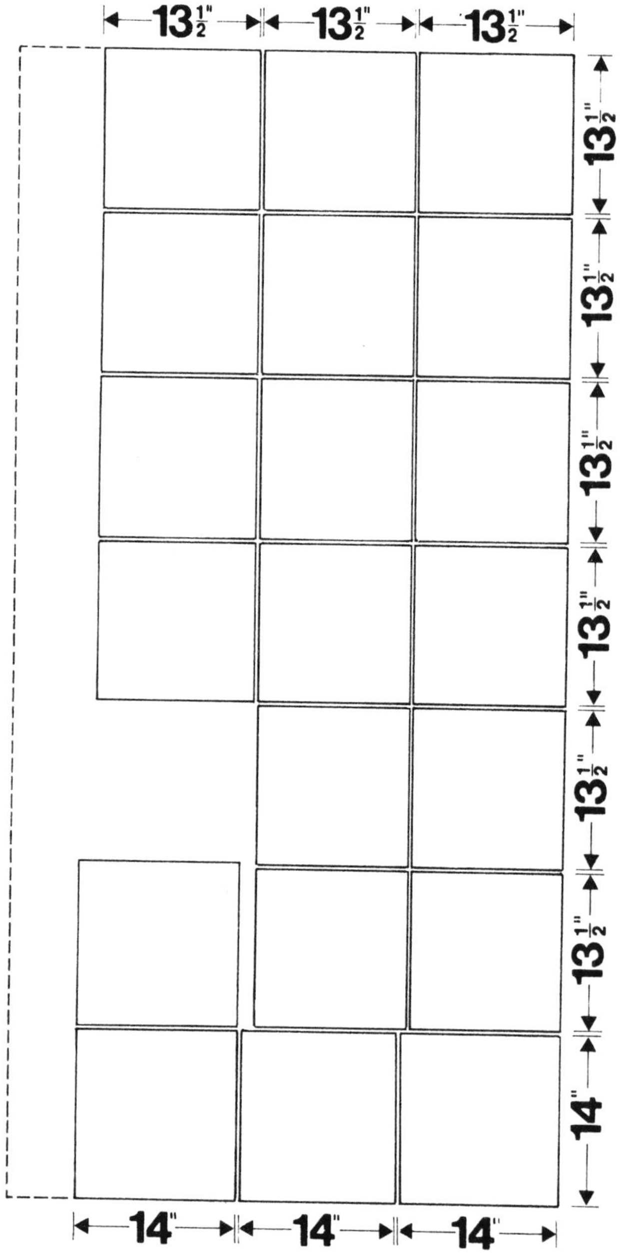

Name

Address

Telephone

Order No. 19

Please supply
one 8′ x 4′ sheet of ½″ plywood cut as shown

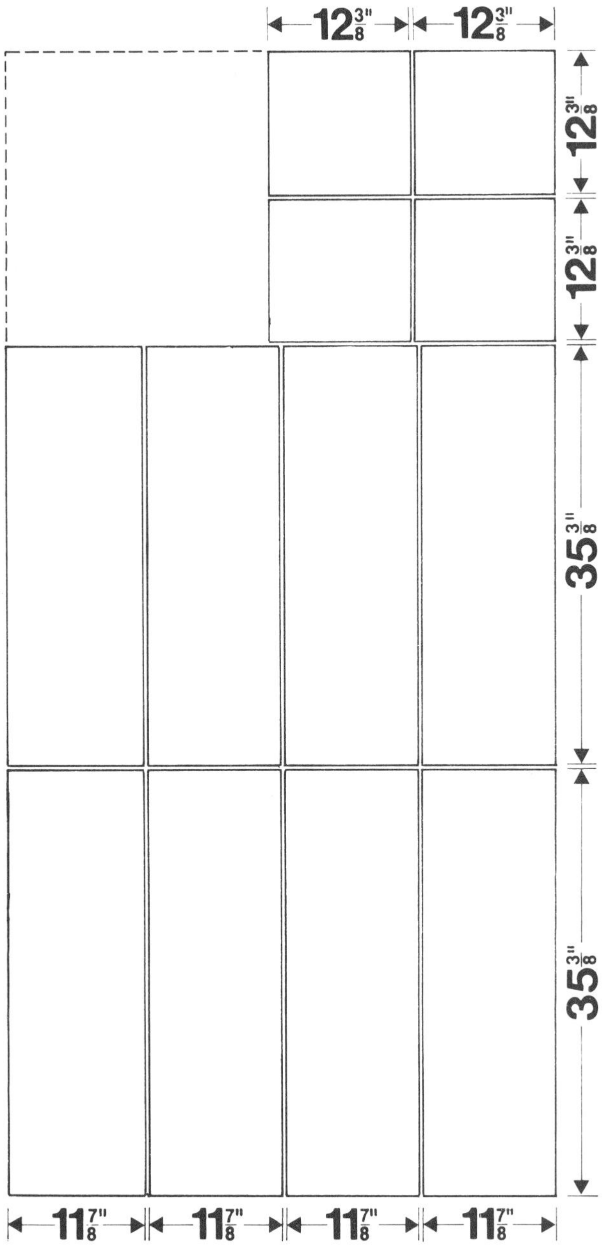

Name

Address

Telephone

$12\tfrac{3}{8}''$ $12\tfrac{3}{8}''$

$12\tfrac{3}{8}''$

$12\tfrac{3}{8}''$

$35\tfrac{3}{8}''$

$35\tfrac{3}{8}''$

$11\tfrac{7}{8}''$ $11\tfrac{7}{8}''$ $11\tfrac{7}{8}''$ $11\tfrac{7}{8}''$

Order No. 20

Please supply
one 8' x 4' sheet of ¾″ plywood cut as shown

Name _____

Address _____

_____

Telephone _____

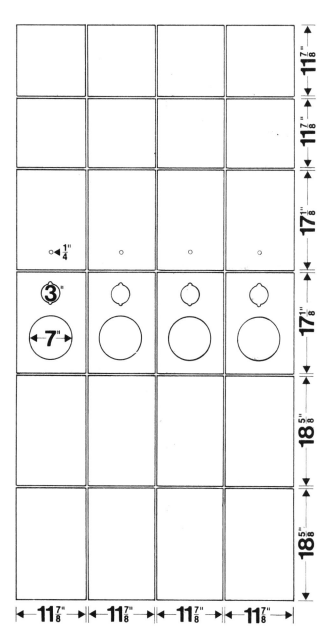

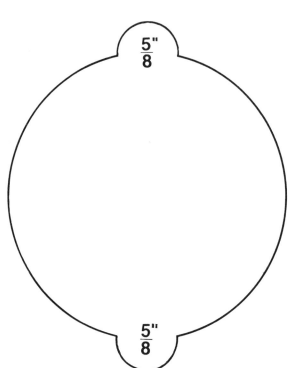

Actual size detail of 3″ hole

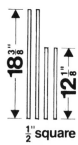

Please supply
one 8' x 4' sheet of ¾" plywood cut as shown

Please supply
one 8' x 4' sheet of ¼" plywood cut as shown

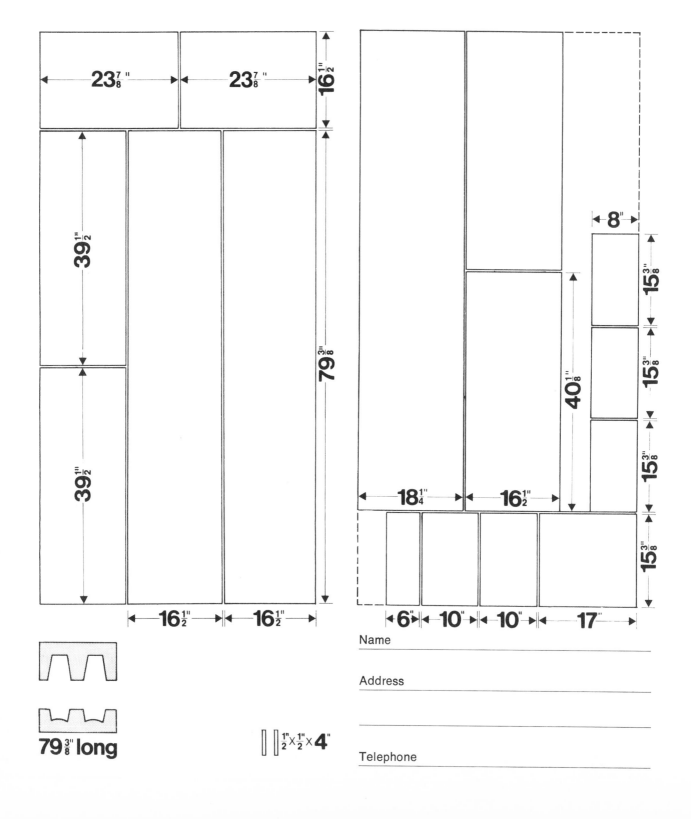

Name

Address

Telephone

Please supply
one 8′ x 4′ sheet of ¾″ plywood cut as shown

Name

Address

Telephone

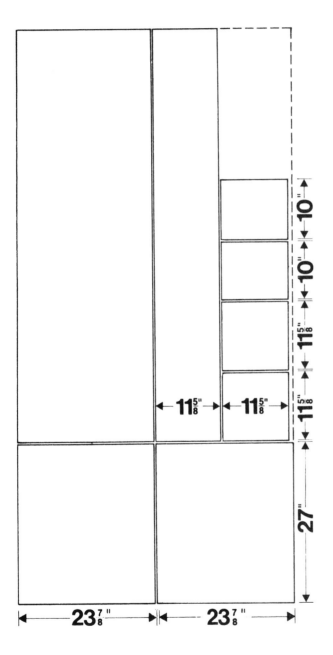

Order No. 23

Please supply
three 8' x 4' sheets of ½" plywood cut as shown

Please supply two 8' x 4' sheets of ¾" plywood cut as shown

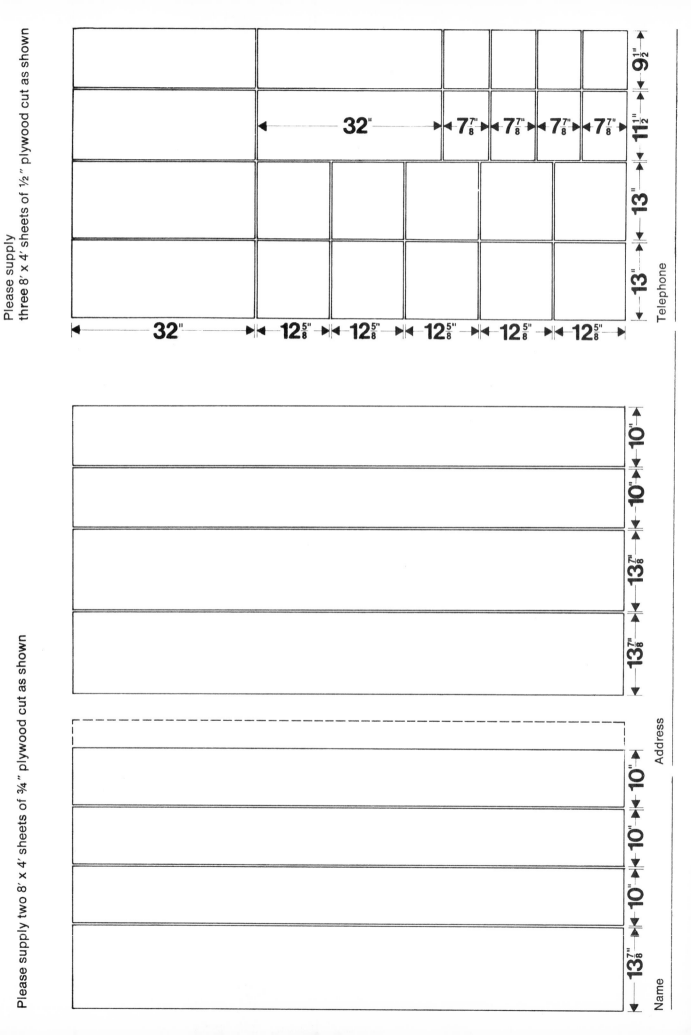

Name

Address

Telephone

Centering Ruler

Cut out the three parts of this ruler and glue them together so that the numbers progress from the center in both directions. Glue this on cardboard.

The centering ruler is used to find the position of the center brace on the side panel of the stools or the top of the tables. Lay the ruler across the panel, adjusting it until the values at both edges are the same. The shaded brown square will then indicate the position of the center brace.

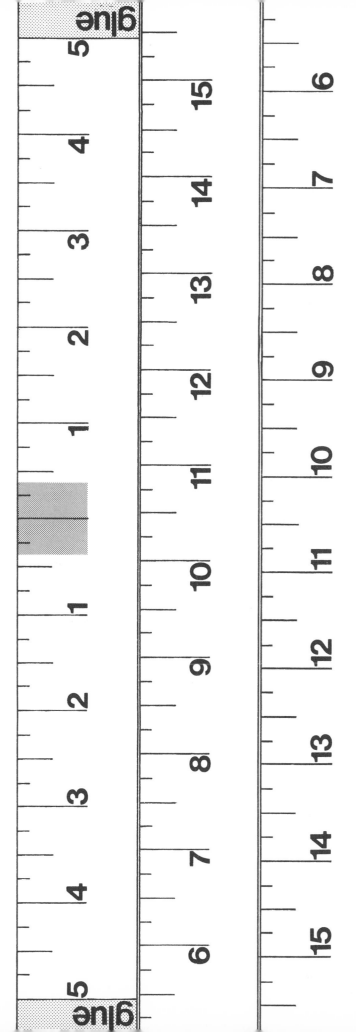